I0759533

OMAR SULEIMAN

# Servants of the Most Merciful

Servants of the Most Merciful

*First published in England* by Kube Publishing Ltd
Markfield Conference Centre Ratby Lane,
Markfield Leicestershire,
LE67 9SY
United Kingdom
Tel: +44 (0) 1530 249230
Website: www.kubepublishing.com
Email: info@kubepublishing.com

 Cataloguing-in-Publication Data is available from the British Library.

ISBN 978-1-84774-269-8 Casebound
eISBN 978-1-84774-270-4 Ebook

*Proofreading and editing:* Quillspire
*Cover design and typesetting:* Afreen Fazil (Jaryah Studio)
*Printed by:* IMAK Ofset, Turkey.

# Contents

# Introduction

In this book, we will explore the concept of "*ʿibād al-Raḥmān*", or "servants of the Most Merciful", and analyse the profound characteristics we are told this exceptional group of servants possess. The term is taken from a beautiful passage in the Qurʾān that offers believers a comprehensive guide to living a life of purpose and meaning. It spans the full spectrum of human experience—from the intimate moments of *qiyām al-layl* (night prayer) in the corner of one's room, to public dealings in a courtroom, to even the seemingly mundane moments of life.

Before delving into the characteristics detailed in these verses, we must first understand the significance of the title Allah ﷾ bestows upon the *ʿibād al-Raḥmān*. Allah ﷾ says in the Qurʾān:

وَعِبَادُ الرَّحْمَٰنِ الَّذِينَ يَمْشُونَ عَلَى الْأَرْضِ
هَوْنًا وَإِذَا خَاطَبَهُمُ الْجَاهِلُونَ قَالُوا سَلَامًا

***The servants of the Most Merciful are those who walk on the earth modestly, and when the ignorant address them, they say, "Peace."***
***[al-Furqān 25:63]***

Many commentators dive straight into elucidating the characteristics of these special people, but before we examine how these servants walk upon the earth, we should first contemplate what it means to be a servant of the Most Merciful. This designation carries weighty implications that even classical *mufassirūn* (exegetes) sometimes pass over too quickly in their haste to discuss the characteristics that follow.

By virtue of our very existence, we are all "*ʿibād*" ("servants") of Allah ﷻ, regardless of whether we acknowledge this reality or not. We exist in a state of inevitable servitude to our Creator. However, there exists a special category of people who consciously embrace this servitude and actively strive to manifest their submission to Allah ﷻ in accordance with His Divine pleasure. These are the ones truly honoured with the title *ʿibād al-Raḥmān*.

This concept is echoed in Sūrah al-Muʾminūn, whose opening *āyāt* (verses) describing the believers mirror the closing passages of Sūrah al-Furqān that we will study in this text. It is no coincidence that the two passages appear in close proximity within the Qurʾān, weaving together a tapestry of Divine guidance.

What characteristics elevate a person to the station of *ʿibād al-Raḥmān*? Allah ﷻ details a clear contrast between the conduct of the believers and that of the disbelievers and Hypocrites. The influence of being servants of the Most Mercial manifests in observable behaviour, with the Prophet Muḥammad ﷺ standing as the ultimate exemplar of these qualities. His noble character serves as a living testament to the transformative power of Divine revelation.

As a wise man once stated, "Be callers to Allah ﷻ even in your silence." This calling is achieved through the beauty of one's character. When people witness the distinct qualities of the believer, it naturally draws them to investigate the source of such noble conduct. Hence, some scholars note that Allah ﷻ enumerates eminently visible characteristics in Sūrah al-Furqān—so that any sincere seeker can readily distinguish between the conduct of the Prophet Muḥammad ﷺ and his followers and that of those who oppose Divine guidance. The contrast is clear, allowing each soul to choose its path with clarity.

In the *āyah* we quoted from Sūrah al-Furqān, why did Allah ﷻ choose to call them the servants of the Most Merciful (the Most Merciful), rather than using any other of His Divine names? This question leads us to a deeper appreciation of the unique status of the name "*al-Raḥmān*". For amongst the beautiful names of Allah ﷻ, *al-Raḥmān* holds a distinction that sets it apart.

Allah ﷻ asks in the Qurʾān:

رَبُّ السَّمَاوَاتِ وَالْأَرْضِ وَمَا بَيْنَهُمَا فَاعْبُدْهُ
وَاصْطَبِرْ لِعِبَادَتِهِ ۚ هَلْ تَعْلَمُ لَهُ سَمِيًّا

***Lord of the Heavens and the earth and everything between them. So worship Him and persevere in His servitude. Do you know of anyone worthy of His name? [Maryam 19:65]***

Indeed, even the idolaters of ancient Arabia, who had no hesitation in appropriating Divine attributes for their idols, never dared to use the name *al-Raḥmān* for any of their deities.

Scholars have pondered the magnitude of the Divine question: “Do you know of anyone worthy of His name?” Some suggest it transcends mere nomenclature, asking instead: “Have you ever encountered any name like *al-Raḥmān*?” or “Does anyone invoke the Most Merciful in the manner that believers do?” Others interpret it as questioning whether any being could be comparable to *al-Raḥmān* in His perfect attributes.

Whenever Allah ﷻ attributes something or someone to Himself, it signifies an elevation in honour. Although being a servant of Allah ﷻ is already the highest honour, being specified as a servant of *al-Raḥmān* carries an additional distinction. Allah ﷻ did not choose to call these people servants of the Most Merciful without a purpose.

What makes this name so special? Unlike many other Divine names, *al-Raḥmān* cannot be attributed to anyone but Allah ﷻ. Other names such as *al-Aḥad* (the Unique) and *al-Ṣamad* (the Eternal Refuge) are also exclusive to Allah ﷻ, whereas *al-Mutakabbir* (the Majestic One), in a human context, carries negative connotations of arrogance, but when attributed to Allah ﷻ, refers to a perfect Divine attribute.

*Al-Raḥmān* belongs to the category of exclusive names. One cannot address another person as *Raḥmān* without preceding the name with "*ʿAbd*" ("servant of"). This differentiates it from Divine names such as *Karīm* (generous), *Ḥakīm* (wise), or *Rashīd* (rightly guided), which, whilst being attributes of Allah ﷻ, can also be used to describe human beings. The exclusivity of *Raḥmān* isn't because humans are incapable of mercy, but rather because the mercy of Allah ﷻ, in all its perfection and completeness, transcends anything His creation could achieve.

This special status is reflected in the statement of the Prophet ﷺ, "The most beloved of your names to Allah ﷻ are ʿAbdullāh and ʿAbd al-Raḥmān" (Sunan Abī Dāwūd 4950). When we name our children, we hope they will embody the qualities their names represent. Thus, the Prophet ﷺ designating these names as the most beloved to Allah ﷻ carries a deep significance.

Scholars note that every characteristic of *ʿibād al-Raḥmān* represents an implementation of mercy in its respective domain. This mercy manifests in relationships, daily interactions, and how we carry ourselves. Being a merciful human necessitates maintaining a humble presence—ensuring that others feel safe from harm through our words and actions—and cultivating trustworthiness.

As the Prophet ﷺ taught us, "The Most Merciful has mercy on those who are merciful. If you show mercy to those who are on the earth, He who is in the Heavens will show mercy to you" (Sunan Abī Dāwūd 4941). The comprehensiveness of the name *al-Raḥmān* is also unique. His mercy encompasses non-believers and believers, the visible and invisible, and this world and the Hereafter.

This differs from *al-Raḥīm* (the Mercifier), which represents a specific, exclusive form of Divine mercy. Whilst *al-Raḥmān* extends to all creation in some measure, *al-Raḥīm* is a special mercy of Allah ﷻ that is reserved for the believers. By contrast, Allah ﷻ is *al-Raḥman* even to those who reject Him, as reflected in the delay of punishment and opportunity for repentance given to unbelievers. We even see the effects of His being *al-Raḥmān* in the natural world—in the gentleness of animals with their young and in every act of mercy between creatures. All mercy in this world, whether acknowledged or not, flows from Him being *al-Raḥmān*.

For us as believers, contemplating and implementing *raḥmah* (mercy) in our interactions becomes essential to our spiritual journey. It forms the foundation of how we engage with all of creation, reflecting in our own limited way the boundless mercy of *al-Raḥmān*.

But what does it mean to be a merciful person? If we were to engage in *tadabbur* (deep reflection) on the concept of mercy, how would it manifest in our daily lives? Consider the various scenarios we encounter: when someone owes us money; when we discover someone's hidden shame; when we enter our homes or community gatherings; when we find ourselves in positions of power over those who once wronged us—what does mercy look like in each of these moments?

We must realise that mercy permeates every aspect of life, including our financial dealings, social interactions, and personal relationships. Even if Allah ﷻ had not enumerated the specific qualities of *ʿibād al-Raḥmān*, the very designation calls us to contemplate how mercy should manifest in these varied situations.

The Prophet ﷺ stands as our supreme example of living mercy. Allah ﷻ describes him in the most comprehensive way in Sūrah al-Anbiyāʾ:

وَمَا أَرْسَلْنَاكَ إِلَّا رَحْمَةً لِّلْعَالَمِينَ

***We did not send you except as a mercy for humankind. [al-Anbiyā 21:107]***

His mercy transcended mere actions—it was evident in his smile that lifted spirits, in how he built others' self-esteem, in his generosity towards both those who asked and those who remained silent. He showed mercy to his enemies and family alike. Even his role as a bearer of Divine guidance represents mercy, for what greater cruelty could there be than leaving humanity without direction and purpose? The Prophet ﷺ served as a conduit of this mercy, with Revelation being the mercy delivered through him.

As servants of the Most Merciful and followers of the man who was a mercy to the world, we must constantly ask ourselves: how are we embodying mercy in our own lives? How does our presence bring mercy into the settings we inhabit? How do our interactions reflect Divine mercy? How do we truly become *ʿibād al-Raḥmān*? As we progress through this book, the answers to these questions should begin to become more clear, in shā Allāh.

The statement of the Prophet ﷺ regarding the beloved names ʿAbdullāh and ʿAbd al-Raḥmān carries an implicit call to embody these qualities. The blessing of bearing such a name lies in striving to live up to its meaning.

When we approach the Qur'ān, we sometimes encounter situations that seem fixed in time—moments where Allah ﷻ praises certain qualities or highlights specific attributes. Our goal in reading these *āyāt* is not to treat the characteristics of *ʿibād al-Raḥmān* as items on a checklist. Instead, we must strive to apply these qualities to the ever-evolving circumstances of the real world, whilst also maintaining our identity as bearers of mercy.

As servants of the Most Merciful, we should not be content with meeting society's current definitions of mercy. The Prophet ﷺ did not merely meet the standards of excellence of his time but redefined them. Rather than matching the prevailing understanding of mercy, he ﷺ transformed it through unprecedented acts of compassion, and we too must strive to transcend conventional expectations of what it means to be merciful.

This elevation of mercy manifests most notably in our treatment of those who lack mercy. How we behave toward those who bring us no worldly benefit is a profound test of character, and choosing to show kindness purely for the sake of Allah ﷻ becomes a means of spiritual refinement.

As we begin to explore these qualities, know that we have barely scratched the surface. The profound examples of our pious predecessors, the *salaf*, who truly embodied these characteristics, await us. Their stories illuminate the practical application of these noble traits, showing us how to transform these teachings from theoretical understanding to lived reality.

# Introduction Summary

## What is the definition of *'Ibād al-Raḥmān*?

Those who are willingly **serving and worshipping** the Most Merciful.

When Allah gives you a title with His name, it's a means of **honoring you.**

## Why *al-Raḥmān*?

This title belongs **only to Allah.**

Only Allah can be called "*al-Raḥmān*" because no one can achieve **all-encompassing mercy** like Him.

Every defined quality of the *'Ibād al-Raḥmān* is an **implementation of mercy.**

*"The merciful will be shown mercy by the Most Merciful. Be merciful to those on the earth and the One in the heavens will have mercy upon you."*

[Sunan at-Tirmidhi 1924]

## How is "*Al-Raḥmān*" different from "*Al-Raḥīm*"?

| ***Al-Raḥmān*** | ***Al-Raḥīm*** |
|---|---|
| Allah's all-encompassing mercy. | Allah's exclusive mercy. |
| Includes believers and disbelievers, the apparent and the Unseen, the dunya and the ākhirah. | Does not include everyone. |
| Humans cannot achieve all-encompassing mercy. | Humans can reflect this type of mercy. |

## Who are the Ultimate *'Ibād al-Raḥmān*?

The Prophet ﷺ known as ***Rahmatan lil 'Aalameen*** (Mercy to All Worlds)

*"We did not send you except as a mercy to the worlds." (21:107)*

## How can we become *ʿIbād al-Raḥmān*?

*THINK*

What does it mean to be merciful? What does *raḥmah* look like in my life? In communities? In the little everyday transactions of life?

*REFLECT*

How am I being merciful? How is my presence more merciful? Are my interactions done in mercy? What does it look like to show *raḥmah*?

*REMEMBER*

We don't just meet standards of mercy that people set. We redefine mercy itself. The Prophet ﷺ redefined mercy and excellence in his time.

*ACT*

Work towards becoming merciful in every aspect of your life. Make *raḥmah* part of your identity.

# CHAPTER 1

# Humility and Gentleness

وَعِبَادُ الرَّحْمَٰنِ الَّذِينَ يَمْشُونَ عَلَى الْأَرْضِ
هَوْنًا وَإِذَا خَاطَبَهُمُ الْجَاهِلُونَ قَالُوا سَلَامًا

***The servants of the Most Merciful are those who walk on the earth modestly, and when the ignorant address them, they say, "Peace."***
***[al-Furqān 25:63]***

Our journey began with the concept of *ʿIbād al-Raḥmān* (servants of the Most Merciful) — a beautiful title that speaks volumes about the character expected of these special servants. Too often, we find ourselves rushing past the acute implications of this bond, eager to list the designation's attributes instead. Many delve immediately into describing how these servants conduct themselves, overlooking the elegance of the title itself: "servants of the Most Merciful".

Allah ﷻ says that these individuals walk modestly upon the earth and respond with peace when confronted by the ignorant. It is easy to gloss over the significance of walking modestly, focusing instead on the response to ignorance, perhaps due to the many stories about our predecessors handling difficult encounters with wisdom and grace. Indeed, any biography of the Rightly Guided Caliphs of early Islam, the Companions, or any of the sages throughout Islamic history reveals this consistent theme—exemplary conduct when faced with taunting or unbecoming behaviour.

However, we should not rush to the response. First, let us ask ourselves what it means to "walk modestly". The implications are significant, particularly in how this mode of movement embodies *raḥmah*. One of the best ways of instilling mercy toward creation is recognising the vast mercy *al-Raḥmān* has shown us. The scholars advise that when anger rises within us, we should redirect that anger inward. When thoughts of revenge surface, we should consider how many times Allah has withheld immediate retribution for our transgressions against His rights. When forgiveness feels difficult, we should remember how readily Allah forgives us.

To walk the earth with *raḥmah* is to comprehend that Allah has shown immense mercy towards us. He has extended His vast mercy in allowing us to tread upon the earth and derive its benefits, and to learn from our missteps. The sins that are an inextricable feature of all Banī Ādam (children of Ādam) are met with the mercy of Allah, as He forgives us and provides time for repentance. This first connection to *al-Raḥmān* manifests in us treating our surroundings with gratitude and thereby acknowledging His mercy.

The distinction between those who walk modestly on

the earth and those who respond to insults with peace is a matter of timing. The former is a proactive stance, reflecting your essence and presence. Your very being should emanate *raḥmah*. Mercy is already a part of your nature. Whenever challenges arise, therefore, forgiveness follows naturally. After encountering those who fall short of noble conduct, however, our *maghfirah* (pardoning) and *ʿafw* (forgiveness) are brought into the equation.

What motivates this behaviour? Just as you traverse this earth with mercy, recognising the extent of the Most Merciful's mercy towards you, you approach with humility. You are humbled by the mercy of Allah ﷻ upon your very essence.

You are also compelled to forgive, pardon, and overlook, even after your noble character has been violated, by an intense desire for the forgiveness of Allah ﷻ. Recall the ḥadīth which taught us that the Most Merciful shows mercy to those who show mercy on earth. You hope that Allah ﷻ includes you amongst those upon whom mercy descends, and so you work to become among those who are, themselves, merciful.

Nevertheless, it is important to stipulate that the mercy that you show does not excuse *ẓulm* (oppression). Nothing we have mentioned provides license for accepting abusive situations in which other people are harmed—that is a separate discussion altogether.

The scholars begin their analysis of "walking upon the earth" with a literal reading. How one walks and carries themselves can reveal much about their character, particularly in certain cultures. Hence, Luqmān counseled his son:

وَاقْصِدْ فِي مَشْيِكَ وَاغْضُضْ مِنْ صَوْتِكَ ۚ
إِنَّ أَنْكَرَ الْأَصْوَاتِ لَصَوْتُ الْحَمِيرِ

***Moderate your stride, and lower your voice. The most repulsive of voices is the donkey's voice. [Luqmān 31:19]***

Imām Al-Ḥasan al-Baṣrī explained that in prayer, when the heart achieves humility, all limbs embody that same humility and stillness. Therefore, humility should permeate your entire being: your body language, how you look at people, and how you walk towards or past them. All should manifest the mercy you have received from your Lord ﷻ.

When we speak of walking upon the earth with humility, we must note that it encompasses far more than a physical movement. We learn from the Prophet ﷺ that *tawāḍuʿ* (humility) is displayed in every aspect of our presence—how we direct our attention, how we speak to others, and even in the way we choose to ignore certain matters. These subtle demonstrations of character are deeply connected to the concept of humility.

When Allah ﷻ speaks of *ʿibād al-Raḥmān*, He emphasises observable characteristics—qualities that would allow any onlooker to distinguish between the behaviour of oppressors like Abū *Jahl* and Abū Lahab and the noble conduct of Companions such as Abū Bakr ؓ and ʿAbd al-Raḥmān ibn ʿAwf ؓ. These external manifestations serve as clear signs of who embodies Divine guidance and who does not.

The Prophet ﷺ taught us that beyond physical appearances lies the crucial matter of intention and attitude. ʿAbdullāh ibn ʿUmar ؓ told us that the Prophet ﷺ said, "Whilst a man was walking, dragging his dress with pride, he was caused to be swallowed by the earth, and will go on sinking in it till the Day of Resurrection" (Ṣaḥīḥ al-Bukhārī 3485).

Compare this Abū Bakr al-Ṣiddīq ؓ, who, due to his narrow waistline, sometimes had his thawb dragging along the ground. ʿAbdullāh ibn ʿUmar ؓ narrated that the Prophet ﷺ said, "Whoever allows his lower garment to drag out of vanity will find that Allah ﷻ will not look at him on the Day of Resurrection." Abū Bakr ؓ replied, "O Messenger of Allah! My lower garment keeps sliding down, even though I take care to pull and wrap it." The Prophet ﷺ said, "You are not one of those who do it out of vanity" (Riyāḍ al-Ṣāliḥīn 790).

This distinction led to scholarly discussion regarding whether dragging one's garment out of pride constitutes a major sin and whether the unintentional falling of a garment below the ankles carries the same ruling. This particular *fiqhī* discussion deserves its own treatment, which is beyond our remit here. However, the contrast between the man who was swallowed by the earth and Abū Bakr reflects the paramount significance of intention in all matters.

ʿĀʾishah, Mother of the Believers and daughter of Abū Bakr, once observed a man walking as though severely ill, his movements suggesting extreme fatigue. Upon inquiring about his condition, she was told he was one of the *qurrāʾ* (reciters) and that he was exhausted from night prayers.

This response deeply troubled ʿĀʾishah, who had witnessed the conduct of the early Muslims. The *salaf* (first three generations of Muslims) were known to deliberately project strength in their voices and maintain upright postures to avoid any suggestion they had spent their nights in prayer. If they happened to witness any event during the night hours, they would attribute their wakefulness to reasons other than worship. Even when fasting, they would avoid any appearance of hunger to prevent others from thinking highly of them.

ʿĀʾishah took particular exception to those who would make their worship apparent through exaggerated displays. Modern-day examples might include: "Why are you sleepy at work?" "I was praying *tahajjud* all night, mā shāʾ Allāh." "Why is your posture poor?" "Those eight *rakʿāt* of prayer every night really affect my back." "Why are your eyes red?" "I was crying all night, mā shāʾ Allāh." When she saw the man walking as though debilitated by worship, ʿĀʾishah remembered ʿUmar and said, "May Allah have mercy on ʿUmar. He was one of the leaders among the reciters, yet his worship never diminished his dignified bearing" (Al-Kāmil fī al-Lughah wa al-Adab 2/122).

What does this tell us about humility? Humility is an internal state and not something we should display to the world. Walking humbly on the earth does not mean appearing weak or feeble. Rather, one should walk with dignity and grace. Arrogance or haughtiness, however, should never be reflected in our gait.

When ʿĀʾishah spoke of ʿUmar, she painted a picture of complete authenticity. Though he spent his nights in Qurānic recitation, his steps remained purposeful and strong. His voice carried clearly when he spoke, showing no sign of exhaustion. When he struck, it was with might, and when he provided food—despite his own home's modest means—he did so with generosity.

His brisk walking may even have been mistaken for pride, though it was far from such a thing.

In every era, pride takes different forms. In those times, it might have been tribal affiliation, physical prowess, or fame. Today, it might be cars or social status. Yet religious pride, masquerading as false humility, remains perhaps the most insidious form of ostentation. Those who affect a deliberately slow or humble walk, attempting to display their piety, are merely engaging in another form of showing off.

Consider ʿUmar ibn *ʿAbd* al-ʿAzīz ﵀. He was raised amongst the nobles of the Banī Umayyah who were taught a particular way of walking. When questioned about his swift pace, he apologised, explaining that it was how he had beeen taught to walk. Remarkably, he then strived to unlearn this gait, which he viewed as carrying traces of pride!

Consider also the *shamāʾil* (virtues) of the Prophet ﷺ, whose walk was neither too fast nor too slow. He walked with purpose but without conceit, requiring others to keep pace yet remaining free of arrogance.

Allah ﷻ speaks of those who walk *hawnan* (humbly) upon the earth. The scholars note a profound reminder in the mention of the earth here: we walk upon that from which we were created. As Allah ﷻ says:

مِنْهَا خَلَقْنَاكُمْ وَفِيهَا نُعِيدُكُمْ
وَمِنْهَا نُخْرِجُكُمْ تَارَةً أُخْرَىٰ

***From it, We created you. And into it, We will return you. And from it, We will bring you out another time.***
***[Ṭā Hā 20:55]***

Each step we take upon the earth is a step upon both our origin and resting place. This reality highlights our essence before Allah ﷻ. Created from earth as descendants of Ādam ﷺ, who was made from *turāb* (dust), our humility before *al-Raḥmān* teaches us two vital lessons. First, regarding our personal essence: people often grow arrogant when they forget their origins. We rise from the earth yet never truly leave it, remaining bound to it until we return to it in burial, and this connection to the earth should remind us of our humble beginnings. Allah ﷻ explains that we were produced from *nutfah*, an insignificant fluid. Once formed, we learn to walk, but must do so upon the very ground from which our species originated.

The second lesson concerns our relationship with the world and its inhabitants—all of us were created from Ādam ﷺ, and Ādam ﷺ was created from dust. There is no room for pride, and worldly distinctions mean nothing before Allah ﷻ. Only *taqwā*

(God-consciousness), residing in the heart, truly distinguishes us. We should never look down upon others based on race, gender, education, wealth, or status. Just as we share a common origin, we will share the same return. Before Allah ﷻ, we stand equal except in our consciousness of Him.

The person before you, regardless of their station, is fashioned from the same substance, will return to the same earth, and will face Allah ﷻ in the same way as you. On that day, only good deeds will distinguish between souls. This understanding should shape how we carry ourselves—not forcing others to stand up in our presence or making gatherings uncomfortable with our arrival. A humble presence manifests in many small considerations that reflect our recognition of this shared human condition.

Many fail to realise how merely their presence can carry expectation, how their entrance into a room bears significant weight, or how they subconsciously demand service from others. Consider the beautiful example of Mujāhid ؒ, who recalled his numerous lengthy journeys with Ibn ʿUmar ؓ. Though Mujāhid ؒ sought to serve Ibn ʿUmar ؓ—his senior and a major scholar from the Companions—he found himself more often the recipient of service, highlighting the principle of not allowing others to shoulder our personal burdens.

A heavy presence manifests in numerous ways: becoming easily agitated, making others fearful of speaking freely around you, or compelling people to select their words carefully, knowing that your temper could easily ignite. It shows in disrupting gatherings with unnecessary loudness or polluting the environment. We must ask ourselves: what impact does my arrival have in a room full of people? What message does it convey to those present? Is it a humble arrival?

There is a crucial distinction between being honoured for noble characteristics—like ʿUthmān ﵁, whose presence was so respected that even the Prophet ﷺ would straighten up and adjust his garments when he entered a room, citing his shyness around a man whom even the Angels revered—and being feared. The first springs from genuine respect, the second from intimidation.

Consider the subtle presence required with parents. Allah ﷻ proclaims:

وَاخْفِضْ لَهُمَا جَنَاحَ الذُّلِّ مِنَ الرَّحْمَةِ
وَقُلْ رَبِّ ارْحَمْهُمَا كَمَا رَبَّيَانِي صَغِيرًا

***Lower to them the wing of humility, out of mercy, and say, "My Lord, have mercy on them, as they raised me from childhood." [al-Isrāʾ 17:24]***

Subḥān Allāh! Notice the language Allah ﷻ chooses—we have been advised to lower wings of humility, out of mercy. This command connects directly to our identity as *ʿibād al-Raḥmān*. When parents call and a child responds reluctantly, that is an example of a heavy presence. But consider when parents age and require service—how do they experience your care? Is it with the reluctance of "Fine, I'll do this for you," or the honour of "I am privileged to serve you"?

The Prophet ﷺ exemplified subtle presence in his home. When ʿĀ'ishah ؓ was asked about his domestic life, she described him as a simple man who was devoted to his family. He would milk his own sheep, mend his own clothes, shop for his necessities, and dine with his servants. He was the first to offer greetings of *salām* (peace) to others. His humility showed in his simplicity, and he never imposed himself with a heavy manner.

Even in admonishment, his presence remained gentle. Anas ibn Mālik ؓ recalls that the Prophet ﷺ never dealt harshly with him. Anas ؓ spent many years in service of the Prophet ﷺ, and said, "If I did anything, he never asked me why I did it, and if I refrained from doing anything, he never asked me why I refrained from doing it" (Ṣaḥīḥ al-Bukhārī 2768).

When walking upon the earth with humility, you proactively become a source of calm in your environment—greeting with *salām*, offering smiles, putting others at ease, helping with heavy objects, and serving those in your vicinity. Your presence becomes subtle, comforting, and calm, rather than arrogant or boastful, and this serves as the default state for the believer.

ʿĀʾishah ﷺ said about the Messenger of Allah ﷺ that he "never hit anything with his hand—neither a servant nor a woman—but, of course, he did fight in the cause of Allah ﷻ. He never took revenge upon anyone for a wrong done to him, but, of course, he exacted retribution for the sake of Allah ﷻ in instances where the injunctions of Allah ﷻ regarding impermissible matters were violated" (Riyāḍ al-Ṣāliḥīn 643). This is our example. This is the description of the best of creation ﷺ.

# Chapter One Summary

عِبَادُ الرَّحْمَـٰنِ الَّذِينَ يَمْشُونَ عَلَى الْأَرْضِ هَوْنًا

*"Are those who tread the earth lightly..." (25:63)*

## What does it mean to "tread the earth lightly" and with *raḥmāh* (mercy)?

**Your spiritual state:**
Begin with mercy, end with forgiveness.

- You have **internal mercy** with creation because you recognize the unending *raḥmāh* Allah has had with you.
- You treat the world with **gratitude**.
- If you're treated badly, **you're forgiving** because you would want Allah to forgive you. (This is not an excuse for abuse or oppression.)

**Your exterior state:**

*"If the heart is humble, then all the limbs will be humble."*
– *Hasan al-Basri*

- You walk gently and speak softly.
- You carry yourself with humility.
- You regularly **renew your intentions.**
- False humility in faith is a form of showing off (*riya'*).

## Why is the earth mentioned in this verse?

**To remind you that you are from the earth.**

- You're mindful that *al-Raḥmān* created you from dirt.
- To forget your origin is to develop arrogance.

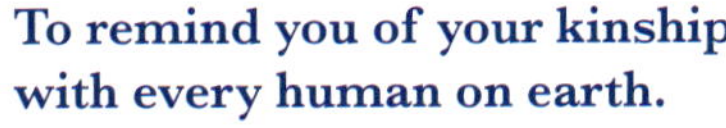

**To remind you of your kinship with every human on earth.**

- None should be belittled based on their race, gender, education, origin, etc.
- In the sight of Allah, the only true distinction between people is *taqwa*.

You are walking on what you are made of.

You **came** from the earth, you'll **return** to it, and you'll be **resurrected** from it.

## What does it mean to have a humble presence?

"Why is your voice so hoarse?"
"Yeah bro, I recited a whole juz' last night you know, nbd."

***"Whoever humbles himself for Allah ﷻ, Allah will raise him by a degree. Whoever is arrogant to Allah by a degree, Allah will lower him by a degree until he is made the lowest of the low."*** *[Sunan Ibn Mājah 4176]*

- Smile
- Initiate *salām*
- Be helpful to others; serve them
- Speak in a comforting tone
- Bring in *brāq* (peace) not fear
- Walk humbly
- Humble yourself to be honored
- Be in the service of your family, especially your parents

- Act harshly
- Speak loudly or angrily
- Make people afraid of you
- Pollute the world or hearts
- Make people go out of their way for you
- Make people uncomfortable with your presence
- Disrespect your parents

## How can we tread lightly on the earth?

***THINK***

When you walk into a room full of people, what effect do you have? Is it positive or negative? Are people happy or uncomfortable?

***REFLECT***

What attitude does your body language suggest? Is your intention to "humble-brag"?

***REMEMBER***

Don't forget where you came from. Your earthly origins should humble you and keep you from arrogance.

***ACT***

Embody mercy, both physically and spiritually. Humble yourself to Allah and serve everyone around you.

CHAPTER 2

# Modesty and Peace

وَعِبَادُ الرَّحْمَٰنِ الَّذِينَ يَمْشُونَ عَلَى الْأَرْضِ
هَوْنًا وَإِذَا خَاطَبَهُمُ الْجَاهِلُونَ قَالُوا سَلَامًا

***The servants of the Most Merciful are those who walk on the earth modestly, and when the ignorant address them, they say, "Peace." [al-Furqān 25:63]***

Allah ﷻ tells us that when the servants of the Most Merciful are addressed by the ignorant, they respond with peace—nothing can disconcert them or remove them from their element.

This introduces the concept of *ḥilm* (forbearance), which scholars declare to be the most challenging virtuous trait to acquire. Whilst being patient, in general, is difficult, it becomes particularly testing when facing direct personal provocation, whether online or in person. Harm and ignorance are harder to bear when they have a face. *Ḥilm* flows from humility; one must be humble to cultivate forbearance.

Allah ﷻ teaches us a crucial sequence: first establish a connection with *al-Raḥmān*, then radiate *raḥmah* towards everything and everyone around you. *Ḥilm* is a form of *raḥmah* that requires humility. Maintaining composure and a mild presence enables forbearance. As the Prophet ﷺ demonstrated, one must maintain a composed and gentle presence, even in the most challenging circumstances.

There are moments when anger should be expressed, when even the Prophet ﷺ left his usual gentle demeanor. However, the impact of such moments lies in their rarity. When one who is known for composure displays anger, people take notice. Conversely, when someone is perpetually angry, others may avoid them simply to escape their constant displeasure. The Prophet ﷺ, as the epitome of humility, patience, and forbearance, made his rare displays of anger deeply meaningful. As the Arabs say, "Fear the anger of a forbearing person," for when such an individual expresses displeasure, it signals something truly serious. Yet, even in anger, the Prophet ﷺ never exceeded the boundaries set by Allah ﷻ.

Abū Hurayrah رضي الله عنه reported the Prophet ﷺ as saying, "Truly, knowledge only comes by learning and forbearance only comes by cultivating forbearance. Whoever aims for good will receive goodness and whoever seeks to evade evil will be protected from it" (Tārīkh Baghdād 9/129). Just as one gains knowledge through study, one cultivates forbearance through daily practice. Managing minor irritations builds a capacity for composure in the face of major trials. Scholars note that the Prophet ﷺ specifically mentioned *ḥilm* (forbearance) highlighting its key significance.

That the Prophet ﷺ declared forbearance attainable through practice suggests that all virtuous traits can be developed similarly. Yet, whilst many engaged in spiritual purification (*tazkiyah*) acquire a number of positive attributes, few successfully overcome a bad temper or transform a harsh demeanor. Doing the latter is particularly difficult. When such harshness is imported into religious practice and causes harm to others, it is especially offensive and ugly.

Allah ﷻ tells us about that when the servants of the Most Merciful are addressed by the ignorant, they say, "Peace." In this statement, the concept of "*jahl*", translated here as "ignorance", is often misunderstood. In classical Arabic poetry, "*jahl*" equates to "*ghaḍab*" (anger). "*Jahl*" was used not to indicate a lack of knowledge (*ʿilm*) but rather the foolish behaviour of one with an ungoverned temper. When Allah ﷻ refers to "*jāhilun*", or "the ignorant", in this *āyah*, He means those who act in anger or foolishness, not those who merely lack knowledge.

This interpretation finds support in Sūrah al-Qaṣaṣ, where Allah ﷻ says:

وَإِذَا سَمِعُوا اللَّغْوَ أَعْرَضُوا عَنْهُ وَقَالُوا لَنَا أَعْمَالُنَا
وَلَكُمْ أَعْمَالُكُمْ سَلَامٌ عَلَيْكُمْ لَا نَبْتَغِي الْجَاهِلِينَ

***And when they hear vain talk, they turn away from it, and say, "We have our deeds, and you have your deeds; peace be upon you; we do not desire the ignorant." [al-Qaṣaṣ 28:55]***

This *āyah* refers to those whom were given the Scripture before the Qur'ān was revealed. Sa'īd ibn Jubayr ﵀ said, "This was revealed concerning seventy priests who were sent by al-Najāshī (the Negus). When they came to the Prophet ﷺ, he recited to them, "Yā Sīn. By the Wise Qur'ān", until he completed the sūrah. They began to weep, and they embraced Islam" (Tafsīr Ibn Kathīr). Elsewhere in the Qur'ān, Allah ﷻ tells us:

وَإِذَا سَمِعُوا مَا أُنزِلَ إِلَى الرَّسُولِ تَرَىٰ أَعْيُنَهُمْ
تَفِيضُ مِنَ الدَّمْعِ مِمَّا عَرَفُوا مِنَ الْحَقِّ ۖ يَقُولُونَ
رَبَّنَا آمَنَّا فَاكْتُبْنَا مَعَ الشَّاهِدِينَ

***And when they hear what was revealed to the Messenger, you see their eyes overflowing with tears, because of the truth they recognise. They say, "Our Lord, we have believed, so count us among the witnesses." [al-Mā'idah 5:83]***

Saʿīd ibn Jubayr ﵀, al-Suddī ﵀, and others said that this was revealed in response to this same delegation.

When Abū Jahl and some of the Quraysh began mocking these converts, as they did with the people of Makkah, the Abyssinian Muslims responded with dignity, saying, "We have our deeds, and you have your deeds; peace be upon you; we do not desire the ignorant." They refused to engage with the taunting, thereby demonstrating true forbearance.

This theme of responding to hostility with peace appears again when Allah ﷻ commands:

خُذِ الْعَفْوَ وَأْمُرْ بِالْعُرْفِ وَأَعْرِضْ عَنِ الْجَاهِلِينَ

***Be tolerant, command decency, and avoid the ignorant. [al-Aʿrāf 7:199]***

The *mufassirūn* (exegetes) relate this statement to an incident involving ʿUyaynah ibn Ḥiṣn ibn Ḥudhayfah ﵀, who stayed with his nephew al-Ḥurr ibn Qays ﵀, a close companion of ʿUmar ibn al-Khaṭṭāb ﵁ due to his status among the *ḥuffāẓ* (preservers) and *qurrāʾ* (reciters) of the Qurʾān.

Ibn ʿAbbās ﵄ reported, "ʿUyaynah ﵀ said to al-Ḥurr ﵀, 'My dear nephew, you have access to the Leader of the Believers. Will you obtain permission for me to sit with him?' Al-Ḥurr asked ʿUmar and he gave permission. When ʿUyaynah came into the presence of ʿUmar, he addressed him, "O son of al-Khaṭṭāb, you neither bestow much on us nor deal with us justly."'ʿUmar got angry and was about to beat him when al-Ḥurr said, 'O Leader of the Believers, Allah has said to his Prophet, "Be tolerant, and command decency, and avoid the ignorant" [al-Aʿrāf 7:199]. This is one of the ignorant ones.' When al-Ḥurr recited this, ʿUmar became motionless in his seat. He always adhered strictly to the Book of Allah" (Riyāḍ al-Ṣāliḥīn 357).

Whilst this was not the original context for the verse's revelation, it beautifully demonstrates its application after the time of the Prophet.

Al-Ḥurr's message was clear; "Do not worry about these people, O Leader of the Believers. They are only trying to provoke you. Turn away from them, for they are not worth your time."

This incident opens up a deeper discussion about how we should respond to provocateurs. The Qurānic term "*al-jāhilūn*" does not refer here, for example, to the Bedouin who approached the Prophet whilst not understanding proper etiquette. Instead, it describes those who are foolish instigators; hot-tempered people who deliberately try to unsettle others.

Three *āyāt* in the Qur'ān address this concept of responding to *al-jāhilīn*, and they all convey the same message: respond with *salām* (peace). But this is not the well-known *salām* of Islamic greetings (*taḥiyyat al-Islām*). Scholars explain this as *salām al-mutāraka wa iʿrāḍ*—the *salām* of disengagement. It is not an invitation to further discussion, but rather a conclusion; a bit like saying, "Peace out." You are signalling that you are not interested in engaging with their provocative behaviour.

We must remember that these *āyāt* do not justify accepting *ẓulm* (oppression). When Allah ﷻ mentions responding to the ignorant with peace, He is specifically addressing discourse with habitually antagonistic individuals who try to disturb you. The guidance here does not indicate accepting abuse, but rather maintaining your composure when faced with provocateurs. When someone tries to provoke you, their victory comes from successfully pulling you down to their level.

Our pious predecessors left us beautiful examples of handling such situations. Al-Ḥasan al-Baṣrī رحمه الله would send gifts of fruit to gatherings where he knew people were backbiting him, saying that he had nothing else to repay them with in this world for the good deeds they were transferring to him in the Hereafter. Perhaps in our modern context, responding to online trolling with fruit emojis might capture that same spirit of dignified disengagement!

These stories show us how to maintain composure without compromising our dignity or accepting genuine injustice. The *salaf* demonstrated that responding to abrasive—though not abusive—individuals requires wisdom, restraint, and the ability to rise above provocation whilst staying true to our principles.

The principle of *qabūl al-ẓulm* (accepting oppression) does not extend to condoning rudeness, particularly when it is gratuitous. Let us examine several illuminating incidents that demonstrate forbearance, beginning with Abū Bakr al-Ṣiddīq ﵁. Whilst we know of instances where he stood up against those who showed ignorance towards the Prophet ﷺ, unable to bear witnessing such behaviour, another incident during his caliphate is particularly revealing.

One day, as Abū Bakr ﵁ sat in the mosque, a man entered and began hurling foul language at him. Abū Bakr ﵁ was the caliph, wielding an authority that would have allowed him to punish this ignorant individual without fear of consequence. This detail is crucial, for people often restrain themselves out of fear rather than true forbearance. A caliph, however, would not have this constraint.

When the man began his tirade, Abū Bakr ﵁ simply stood up and walked away. The man called after him, "Oh Ibn Abī Quḥāfah, I am addressing you! Do not walk away, for my remarks concern you alone!” Abū Bakr responded, “But I am choosing to distance myself from you.” Even when the man threatened him with a curse that he promised would follow him to his grave, Abū Bakr remained composed, replying that such curses would actually accompany their speaker to his grave, not their target.

The man, growing increasingly frustrated, warned that if Abū Bakr spoke another word, he would respond tenfold. Abū Bakr replied, “If you say ten more statements to me, you will not hear a single word in response. I will not engage.” Subḥān Allāh! And with that, he left the mosque, leaving behind a man seething at his failed attempts to provoke him.

Similarly instructive is a story involving ʿUmar ibn ʿAbd al-ʿAzīz, a caliph renowned for his justice and nobility. Once, as he approached the pulpit to deliver a sermon, he accidentally tripped over someone. The man insulted him, asking if he was crazy. ʿUmar simply responded “No” and continued towards the pulpit.

As ʿUmar was preparing for the *khuṭbah* (sermon), he noticed some individuals about to attack the man for his disrespectful remarks, and quickly intervened. “He asked if I was crazy, I said I was not, and that is the end of it,” he declared, exemplifying the principle of turning away from the foolish.

Another striking example is that of Abū Ḥanīfah. During a teaching session, he stated that al-Ḥasan al-Baṣrī, Sayyid al-Tābiʿīn (Leader of the Followers), had made an error in judgement. A man in the mosque, outraged, stood up and shouted "O son of an adulteress!" before storming out. Unperturbed, Abū Ḥanīfah continued his lesson, completing his point that whilst Al-Ḥasan had erred, Ibn Masʿūd was correct on this particular matter. Had the man shown patience, he would have heard the full context—a scholarly discussion comparing the views of a Companion with those of one of the greatest of the followers. Instead, he chose insult and a hasty departure. Abū Ḥanīfah, meanwhile, maintained his composure and simply continued teaching.

Whenever you encounter foolish people who insult you, whether to your face or behind your back, and whether verbally or through writing, the principle remains the same: maintain dignity through disengagement rather than retaliation.

The essence of *ʿibād al-Raḥmān* lies in refusing to descend to the level of those who provoke. Instead, keep your focus on *al-Raḥmān* and remain steadfast despite the provocations of Shayṭān. When Shayṭān attempts to provoke you through others, your singular goal should be gaining the love of *al-Raḥmān*. This is beautifully captured in the Qurānic description:

وَعِبَادُ الرَّحْمَٰنِ الَّذِينَ يَمْشُونَ عَلَى الْأَرْضِ هَوْنًا وَإِذَا خَاطَبَهُمُ الْجَاهِلُونَ قَالُوا سَلَامًا

***The servants of the Most Merciful are those who walk on the earth modestly, and when the ignorant address them, they say, "Peace."* *[al-Furqān 25:63]***

The connection between these two elements—treading lightly and responding peacefully—reveals a crucial understanding. The Prophet ﷺ taught us that true strength does not lie in physically overpowering others but rather in self-control, particularly when anger threatens to overcome you. This composure represents the highest form of strength.

Anas ibn Mālik ؓ witnessed many demonstrations of this remarkable trait. Once, the Prophet ﷺ was strolling when he encountered a harsh, ignorant Bedouin. Anas ؓ reports, "I was walking with the Messenger of Allah ﷺ, and he was wearing a *Najrānī* wrap with a thick border. A Bedouin encountered him and pulled the wrap so violently that I saw traces of wrap's border on the neck of the Messenger of Allah ﷺ. He (i.e. the Bedouin) said, 'Muhammad, order for me to be given from the wealth of Allah at your disposal.' The

Messenger of Allah ﷺ turned his attention to him and smiled, and then ordered for a gift to be given to him" (Ṣaḥīḥ Muslim 1057a).

This moment perfectly demonstrated the epitome of strength—maintaining absolute composure even in the face of crude provocations. This teaching is not about responding to injustice, but rather about adeptly handling those who seek to provoke, instigate, and disturb.

Shayṭān desires precisely the opposite—to unsettle you and compel you to act out of character. If such actions, prompted by losing your composure, lead you away from Allah ﷻ, then Shayṭān has accomplished his goal: to lower you and keep you away from the level of conduct befitting of a person aspiring to be counted amongst *ʿibād al-Raḥmān*.

On the subject of humility, a question often arises about ʿUmar ibn al-Khaṭṭāb ؓ, a man known for his strength and fearlessness: could he too be described as of one those who walks on the earth modestly? The answer is an emphatic yes, for the fear and respect he inspired in others was not caused by his reactions to their words, but rather by reflecting on their own disobedience to Allah ﷻ. It was people's own sins that made them nervous around ʿUmar ؓ, just as ʿUthmān's ؓ virtue made others shy in his presence.

ʿUmar ﵁ was uncompromising when it came to preventing disobedience to Allah ﷻ. Yet, remarkably, a child could advise him to fear Allah ﷻ, and this formidable man would immediately begin weeping. Though his physical presence was imposing—to the point where it was said that Shayṭān would not walk the same path as ʿUmar ﵁—this does not contradict the light gait that characterises *ʿibād al-Raḥmān*. The fact that he was a large, strong, and powerful man is unrelated to what was in his heart. Indeed, his heart would instantly soften at any admonition regarding the rights of Allah ﷻ. He would immediately question his actions, demonstrating profound humility and readiness to hold himself accountable.

Those with a powerful presence should be particularly cautious of allowing their temper to flare in situations where they feel taken advantage of or humiliated. Despite feeling the sting of injustice, you must hold back. Again, this is not to say that a person must tolerate oppression (*ẓulm*), but rather that they should cultivate self-control and develop an awareness of when to either respond or turn away. The pursuit of elevation in the sight of Allah ﷻ requires endurance, and trials are an inevitable part of the journey.

There are times, however, when confronting a bully is essential, particularly if they continue to victimise others. Knowing what to do and when to do it requires careful discernment and wisdom. We must consider whether someone's offensive conduct follows a pattern. For instance, when Muslims are a minority, if they are targeted not due to the perpetrator's generally foul disposition but because of a specific prejudice or racism, then this demands a different response.

The foulness of such bullies differs fundamentally from the behaviour of *al-jāhilūn*, who are indiscriminately rude to everyone they encounter. Unlike *ʿibād al-Raḥmān*, who instil calmness and diffuse tension, they consistently create discomfort and provoke discord. Sometimes, responding to these individuals is necessary not for the sake of ego, but to protect your brothers and sisters in faith and humanity.

This is where discernment becomes crucial. Responding from a place of ego negates any reward, but protecting others represents a noble act, as exemplified by ʿUmar ﵁. The challenge lies in maintaining the correct balance—knowing when to exercise forbearance for personal slights and when to stand firm in defence of yourself and others, all whilst ensuring that your intentions are sincerely for the sake of Allah ﷻ.

Certain incidents in the life of ʿUmar ﵁ might appear to contradict the principle of walking modestly upon the earth. Similarly, acts of self-defence or public correction might seem at odds with the principle of responding to the foolish with peace. Although one should never descend to the level of provocateurs, taking action to protect others or prevent escalating harm is perfectly legitimate. The Qur'ān presents a general principle to live by, but understanding its exceptions requires wisdom. The noble qualities of *ʿibād al-Raḥmān*, which are applicable in usual circumstances, should not be misinterpreted in ways that could enable suffering.

Some people can exhaust one's patience. They are characterised by their ignorance, reckless behaviour, inconsiderate nature, and insensitivity; and the same applies to rudeness encountered in person or online. But instead of becoming riled up by such individuals, picture yourself calmly managing these challenging interactions throughout your day before finding solace in a quiet corner of your home and turning back to Allah ﷻ in worship.

# Chapter Two Summary

وَإِذَا خَاطَبَهُمُ الْجَاهِلُونَ قَالُوا سَلَامًا

*"...and when the jāhilūn address them [harshly], they say [words of] peace..." (25:63)*

## What is *hilm*?

**Forbearance**.

- To be composed, have a mild presence.
- To **practice patience** with people and with the minor irritations of life.
- To only express anger when absolutely necessary and when it will have a **positive impact.**

## Who are the *jāhilūn* in this verse?

Those who act or **speak rudely or foolishly**, who display hot tempers.

In this context, it does not refer to those who are simply ignorant or uneducated.

## What does it mean to say "*salaam*" in this verse?

"Peace out." "I will not engage."

## How did our pious predecessors deal with the *jāhilūn*?

- When they heard any vain talk, they **physically turned away** from it.
- They kept their composure and calmed others, responding with words like:

*"For us are our deeds, and for you are your deeds. Peace will be upon you; we seek not those who are ignorant." (28:55)*

- They **were merciful** and did not punish actions of *jāhilūn* for their own sake, even though they had the authority to do so.

## Lessons from the pious predecessors:

**Act according to the Sight of Allah, not the sight of others.**

- Don't stoop to the level of anyone who attacks you.
- The misdeeds of others, even if directed at you, are not your responsibility.
- Be too focused on *al-Raḥmān* to worry about the provocation of Shaytān.
- Even if you're in a position of power, choose balance and composure over punishment and overreaction.

## Does having *hilm* mean you let people take advantage of you?

*"The strong are not the best wrestlers. Verily, the strong are only those who control themselves when they are angry." [Sahih Muslim 2609]*

- **No**. Sometimes, it will feel unjust to remain silent or leave when you could have raised your voice or said something back.

- *Hilm* also applies to virtual interactions of all types – on social media, in the workplace, etc.
- It's important to **judge wisely** between situations that require a response and those that do not.

**We do not accept oppression.**

For example, when dealing with bigots, racism, or targeted discrimination, it is necessary to respond wisely—**but only to protect others, never to defend your ego or pride.**

## How can we develop *hilm*?

Once we connect to the idea of being *'Ibād al-Raḥmān*, we emanate the *hilm* we seek from Allah and apply it to all areas of our lives, including those in which people may seek to provoke us or make us respond with anger.

### *THINK*

What is Shayṭān trying to make you do? Stop to feel the level of pain when you are rude or harsh. How can you help yourself rise above that impulse?

---

### *REFLECT*

What situations have you faced in which you practiced or failed to practice *hilm*?

---

### *REMEMBER*

You are only responsible for your deeds. If someone acts like a *jāhilūn* with you, it doesn't mean you are responsible for dealing with them. Your goal is to be elevated in the eyes of Allah.

---

### *ACT*

Practice forbearance daily by being patient with small trials. Let the trials in your life not harden you; but soften you. Let it bring light into your heart and mind..

CHAPTER 3

# Prostration and Standing

وَالَّذِينَ يَبِيتُونَ لِرَبِّهِمْ سُجَّدًا وَقِيَامًا

***And those who pass the night before their Lord, prostrating and standing. [al-Furqān 25:64]***

When someone throws a rude remark your way or behaves particularly offensively, yet you respond with grace and restraint, you are drawing on a spiritual strength, an inner reservoir cultivated through worship. To navigate an ever-changing environment effectively, larly in their *ṣalāḥ* (prayer) and *sujūd* (prostrations).

The Prophet ﷺ taught us that, "The believer who mixes with people and endures their harm is better than the one who does neither" (al-Adab al-Mufrad 388). This addresses those who err towards complete seclusion, declaring that they will not participate in community work, mosque-related affairs, organisational tasks, or volunteering. They say they want to focus solely on prayer, meditation, and personal worship—activities they deem more spiritually fulfilling than dealing with people.

This inclination is understandable, as social interactions can be deeply exhausting, especially when dealing with fellow Muslims from whom we expect better conduct.

No matter how many warnings are given, nothing prepares you for the disappointment of witnessing egos interfere in what should be noble, selfless work.

Upon encountering trials and challenges, one might be tempted to withdraw from community engagement entirely, retreating to the comfort of individual worship. Indeed, the Prophet ﷺ found unparalleled joy in his prayer, a pleasure surpassing any satisfaction we could derive from our own. Indeed, he said to Bilāl ﵁, "O Bilāl, proclaim the prayer—give us comfort by it" (Sunan Abī Dāwūd 4985). When describing the night prayer of the Prophet ﷺ, 'Ā'ishah ﵂ speaks of a man completely devoted to Allah ﷻ. She advised, "Do not leave the night prayer, for the Messenger of Allah ﷺ never left it. If he was unwell or felt lethargic, he would pray sitting" (Sunan Abī Dāwūd 1307).

Yet despite the deep satisfaction he derived from prayer, the Prophet ﷺ recognised that enduring the challenges of community service was itself a form of worship. Whether tolerating a rough Bedouin, someone knocking at his door in the middle of the night, or interruptions during his gatherings, he viewed each inconvenience as a form of *ʿibādah*. He patiently bore the difficulties that accompany community service, understanding them as an integral part of serving Allah ﷻ.

Allah ﷻ presents this balanced perspective in these *āyāt*. Those who serve others, pursue good deeds, and carry out permissible daily activities are also performing acts of worship. When they encounter the ignorant or foolish, they simply respond with "*salām*"—expressing their disinterest in associating with negativity. When situations turn unpleasant, they choose dignified disengagement whilst maintaining their commitment to serving the community.

A hallmark of the *ʿibād al-Raḥmān* is not complete withdrawal from societal disputes but rather mindful disengagement from situations that offer no benefit. They step away not from worthwhile endeavors but rather the petty disagreements and ego clashes that plague community work. Their focus remains steadfastly on productivity and benefit, avoiding any contribution to discord and strife, whilst fostering healthy, constructive interactions with others. When they have the ability to prevent discord, they do so, but their primary goal is to interact with people in ways that bring about good.

This discerning approach might mean certain community tasks are not suitable for them—for example, roles that regularly expose them to conflict or require constant navigation of political tensions. Yet, rather than abandon community service entirely, they seek other avenues of beneficial work, embodying the teaching of the Prophet ﷺ, "The best of people are those who are most beneficial to others" (al-Muʿjam al-Awsaṭ li-l-Ṭabarānī 5937). Their aim through their community efforts, therefore, is to attain greater rewards and reach a higher station with their Lord ﷻ.

But how does one maintain dignity and patience in the face of these challenges? How does one build the spiritual fortitude to withstand daily trials whilst remaining productive? The answer is: through their standing and prostrating before their Lord ﷻ in the privacy of night. These servants find their strength in the depths of darkness, when they stand alone before Allah ﷻ, reminding themselves of what truly matters. Through these private moments of devotion, they recharge and rejuvenate their spirits, preparing themselves to greet each new day ready to give from both their wealth and their very selves.

Scholars note that this nightly devotion to prayer also means that these individuals avoid the frivolous night-time activities and wicked deeds often associated with the *sufahāʾ* (foolish ones), whom they so gracefully bear during the day. They do not spend their nights in idle gossip or wasteful pursuits, instead using these precious hours to build their connection with Allah ﷻ.

This brings us to a crucial point about the danger of *riyāʾ* (showing off) through false humility. When discussing those who walk modestly upon the earth—we must be mindful that some people adopt an affected humble gait merely for show. There are those who make their night vigils obvious through an exaggerated sluggish walk the next day, betraying the very essence of sincere worship.

Ibn al-Qayyim ﷺ provides an insight into this phenomenon when discussing taqṣīr al-thawb (shortening the garment). He notes how some perform this action not out of genuine adherence to the Sunnah, but as a means of boasting—precisely what the Prophet ﷺ condemned in those who would drag their garments out of pride.

This same principle extends into how we deal with the foolish among us. If one responds to a foolish or arrogant person with the intention of humiliating them publicly, seeking to elevate oneself through their degradation, then this too constitutes *riyāʾ*. When your intention in handling difficult people becomes showcasing your own cleverness or earning public praise for your patience whilst making others look foolish, then you have strayed far from the path of sincere service.

True humility must emanate from within, something you earnestly seek as a *manzil* (station) with Allah ﷻ. It should represent genuine forbearance born of sincere devotion, not a calculated display designed to diminish others or portray them as fools in public. When someone loses control or acts inappropriately, your self-control should flow naturally from your character, requiring no conscious performance or public recognition.

People might observe and say, "Mā shā' Allāh! Look how they never respond, always maintaining their composure", but this recognition should never be your aim. The Prophet ﷺ said, "A person who pretends that he has been given that which he has not been given is like the one who wears two garments of falsehood" (Ṣaḥīḥ al-Bukhārī 5219). Such a person is not engaging in virtuous actions to seek the pleasure of Allah ﷻ. Rather, they are performing them for worldly advantages, thereby defeating the very purpose of worship and service.

So far, we have examined the first two *āyah*s regarding the *ʿibād al-Raḥmān*:

وَعِبَادُ الرَّحْمَٰنِ الَّذِينَ يَمْشُونَ عَلَى الْأَرْضِ هَوْنًا وَإِذَا
خَاطَبَهُمُ الْجَاهِلُونَ قَالُوا سَلَامًا ۝ وَالَّذِينَ يَبِيتُونَ
لِرَبِّهِمْ سُجَّدًا وَقِيَامًا

***The servants of the Most Merciful are those who walk on the earth modestly, and when the ignorant address them, they say, "Peace." And those who pass the night before their Lord, prostrating and standing. [al-Furqān 25:63-64]***

Scholars suggest that the Qurānic transition from describing the *ʿibād al-Raḥmān* to discussing night worship serves to discourage these servants from engaging in sinful behaviour when away from public view. This is an exhortation to *ikhlāṣ* (sincerity) and overcoming *riyāʾ* (showing off) through genuine devotion to Allah ﷻ. The servants of the Most Merciful maintain their composure through a deep love for Allah ﷻ, whether whilst engaging with others in the light of day or refining themselves in the solitude of night.

Their strength emanates from this sincere connection with their Lord ﷻ, transforming both their private worship and public conduct. This is how *ʿibād al-Raḥmān* generate and maintain their resilience—not through external shows of piety or calculated displays of patience, but through a genuine, internal transformation that naturally manifests in all their dealings. They work continuously on their intentions, understanding that the ultimate goal is not public recognition but the pleasure of Allah ﷻ.

In the quiet moments of the night, they rebuild their spiritual fortitude, enabling them to navigate challenges during the day. Their night worship becomes the foundation of their public service, each supporting and reinforcing the other in a cycle of sincere devotion. They maintain this balance through a constant renewal of their connection with Allah ﷻ, allowing them to serve His creation with humility and steadfastness. Whilst others sleep, they struggle with their own desire for rest, as Allah ﷻ says:

تَتَجَافَىٰ جُنُوبُهُمْ عَنِ الْمَضَاجِعِ يَدْعُونَ
رَبَّهُمْ خَوْفًا وَطَمَعًا وَمِمَّا رَزَقْنَاهُمْ يُنْفِقُونَ

***Their sides shun their beds, as they pray to their Lord, out of reverence and hope; and from Our provisions to them, they give. [al-*Sajdah *32:16]***

They exert significant effort to abandon the comfort of sleep, striving instead to maintain their connection with their Lord ﷻ.

Interestingly, the dignity and obedience displayed during daylight hours can serve as a catalyst for night worship. As one of the *salaf* said, when asked why some struggle to rise for the night prayer, "Do not disobey Him during the day, and He will awaken you at night." *Qiyām al-Layl* is a Divine gift, bestowed upon those dear to Allah ﷻ, those He wishes to honour with His proximity. If one spends their day in foolish conduct, they should not expect to be blessed with night worship. Obedience during daily interactions at work and with others can become a means for Allah ﷻ to awaken you during the night.

Allah ﷻ mentions how some people, when called to prostrate to *al-Raḥmān*, are sceptical:

وَإِذَا قِيلَ لَهُمُ اسْجُدُوا لِلرَّحْمَٰنِ قَالُوا وَمَا الرَّحْمَٰنُ أَنَسْجُدُ لِمَا تَأْمُرُنَا وَزَادَهُمْ نُفُورًا

***And when it is said to them, "Prostrate before the Most Merciful," they say, "And what is the Most Merciful? Are we to prostrate before whatever you command us?" And it increases them in aversion. [al-Furqān 25:60]***

The resistance of such people only increases their aversion to the truth. Those who aspire to be among *ʿibād al-Raḥmān*, however, hold an entirely different perspective. Allah ﷻ says about this noble group:

وَالَّذِينَ يَبِيتُونَ لِرَبِّهِمْ سُجَّدًا وَقِيَامًا

***And those who pass the night before their Lord, prostrating and standing. [al-Furqān 25:64]***

During the SARS CoV-2 quarantine periods, many people waited anxiously for the restrictions to be lifted. The believers, however, found solace in solitude. In this *āyah*, "before their Lord" refers to taking refuge at home with their Lord ﷻ, cherishing private moments of communion. A true believer transforms isolation into spiritual practice, monotony into enrichment, and separation from creation into an opportunity to strengthen their bond with the Creator. Allah ﷻ remains accessible whether we are at home, in the mosque, at work, or driving—He is ever-present. Thus, the believer spends their nights immersed in this relationship with Allah ﷻ.

Allah ﷻ says about a certain group of people:

إِذَا تُتْلَىٰ عَلَيْهِمْ آيَاتُ الرَّحْمَٰنِ خَرُّوا سُجَّدًا وَبُكِيًّا

***Whenever the revelations of the Most Merciful were recited to them, they would fall down, prostrating and weeping. [Maryam 19:58]***

The passage we are studying from Sūrah al-Furqān speaks praisingly about the servants of the Most Merciful. One of the first attributes mentioned is their commitment to the night prayer. They attain honour through their humility before Allah ﷻ. As the Prophet ﷺ taught us, "Charity does not decrease wealth, no one forgives another except that Allah ﷻ increases his honour, and no one humbles himself for the sake of Allah ﷻ except that Allah ﷻ raises his status" (Ṣaḥīḥ Muslim 2588). The Prophet ﷺ also said, "The closest that a person can be to his Lord, the Mighty and Sublime, is when he is prostrating, so increase in supplication at that time" (Sunan al-Nasāʾī 1137).

In *sujūd*, you whisper into the earth and the Most High hears you, honours you, and elevates you. No moment brings you closer to Allah ﷻ. This correlation between *al-Raḥmān* and the act of prostration will come up again.

Scholars explain that *sujūd*, the physical act of humbling and prostrating oneself before Allah ﷻ (*khuḍūʿ*), precedes the internal state of humility (*khushūʿ*). The physical act serves as a gateway to acquiring the internal state, which is characterised by tears and a spiritual transformation. This progression brings one ever closer to Allah ﷻ.

After speaking about those who would fall down prostrating and weeping upon hearing the revelations of the Most Merciful, Allah ﷻ says:

فَخَلَفَ مِنْ بَعْدِهِمْ خَلْفٌ أَضَاعُوا الصَّلَاةَ
وَاتَّبَعُوا الشَّهَوَاتِ ۖ فَسَوْفَ يَلْقَوْنَ غَيًّا

***But they were succeeded by generations who abandoned the prayer and followed their desires. They will face perdition.***
***[Maryam 19:59]***

ʿUmar رضي الله عنه interpreted this as the loss of both *khuḍūʿ* and *khushūʿ*—neglecting the physical humility of *sujūd* through delayed prayers whilst replacing the internal desire for Allah ﷻ with worldly lusts. May Allah ﷻ protect us from such a fate.

There is a subtle beauty in how the physical lowering of oneself aligns with spiritual ascension, creating an intimate connection with the Lord of the Heavens ﷻ. This recalls our earlier point about those who walk upon the earth whilst realising they were created from it—a constant reminder of our inherent humility and earthly connection. In *sujūd*, we return to our origin, pressing our foreheads against the very substance from which we were made, whilst our spirits rise to their highest station before our Lord ﷻ.

Our feet remain perpetually bound to the earth, physically tethered to its surface. Yet amongst all creation, only a select few choose to place their foreheads and faces upon this soil in reverence to the One who made both it and them.

Allah ﷻ says:

وَمِنَ اللَّيْلِ فَاسْجُدْ لَهُ وَسَبِّحْهُ لَيْلًا طَوِيلًا

***And during the night, prostrate to Him, and glorify Him long into the night. [al-Insān 76:26]***

Prostration finds its deepest meaning during the night. Whilst we certainly prostrate throughout the day, with *sujūd* forming an integral part of both our obligatory and sunnah prayers, Allah ﷻ specifically mentions prostrations during the night; referring to these spiritually intense moments. He instructs us to prostrate to Him and glorify Him extensively during these hours.

Special significance is givent to *qiyām al-layl* (the night vigil). When engaging in *sujūd* (prostration) during the night vigil, we should set aside ample time for unscripted supplication. During these precious moments, one can make *duʿāʾ* in any language or manner their heart desires.

There are further secrets of *sujūd* that one may unravel. Allah ﷻ tells us that prostration possesses healing properties for those pained by the words of others. He says:

وَلَقَدْ نَعْلَمُ أَنَّكَ يَضِيقُ صَدْرُكَ بِمَا يَقُولُونَ ۝ فَسَبِّحْ بِحَمْدِ رَبِّكَ وَكُن مِّنَ السَّاجِدِينَ

***We are aware that your heart is distressed by what they say. So glorify the praises of your Lord, and be among those who prostrate. [al-Ḥijr 15:97-98]***

Subḥān Allāh! Allah ﷻ addresses the Prophet ﷺ here, acknowledging his human susceptibility to the emotional pain that results from slander. We must not pretend to be invulnerable—insults, provocations, and defamatory remarks can indeed wound us.

Such sensitivity exists because this is how Allah ﷻ designed our nature. The Prophet ﷺ possessed a magnificent heart and held immense love for people. Consequently, it pained him deeply to be maligned and disparaged by the very individuals he cherished and sought to guide. Allah ﷻ acknowledges this, stating that He knows such remarks brought distress to the heart of the Prophet ﷺ. The Divine prescription?

فَسَبِّحْ بِحَمْدِ رَبِّكَ وَكُنْ مِنَ السَّاجِدِينَ

***So glorify the praises of your Lord, and be among those who prostrate.* *[al-Ḥijr 15:98]***

*Sujūd* holds healing powers. When one thinks deeply about those who cause hurt or inflict pain, or considers the vexations of human interaction, they should remember the potential for healing in prostration. Extended periods of *sujūd* can prove deeply restorative. The Prophet ﷺ also instructed us to perform *sujūd al-shukr* (prostrations of gratitude). Consequently, *sujūd* becomes our refuge in both anguish and joy, and in both hardship and gratitude. It flows from *tawbah* (repentance) and thankfulness to Allah ﷻ for teaching us how to worship Him.

Ibn al-Qayyim ﷺ noted that even the house of worship is each called a masjid—literally, a place of *sujūd*. It is as though the entire prayer serves as preparation for the moment of prostration, with each *rakʿah* building toward this pinnacle. Therefore, when striving to maintain *khushūʿ*, remember that we do not need to merely maintain focus for a few *āyāt* before losing concentration. Rather, we should be building towards the blessed moment of falling into prostration before Allah ﷻ.

The significance of this act extends to the Day of Judgement itself. Rabīʿah ibn Kaʿb al-Aslamī ﷺ said, "I spent the night with the Messenger of Allah ﷺ, and I brought him water for his ablutions and needs. The Prophet ﷺ said to me, 'Ask.' I replied, "I ask for your companionship in Paradise." The Prophet ﷺ said, 'And anything else besides that?' I said, "That is all." The Prophet said, 'Then assist me in achieving that for you by prostrating often'" (Ṣaḥīḥ Muslim 489).

Indeed, on the Day of Judgement, the highest honour of the Prophet ﷺ will be al-Shafāʿah al-ʿUẓma (The Great Intercession), when he will prostrate to Allah ﷻ and be inspired with words previously unknown to him. Yet, on that day, there also lies the gravest humiliation for some:

يَوْمَ يُكْشَفُ عَنْ سَاقٍ وَيُدْعَوْنَ إِلَى السُّجُودِ فَلَا يَسْتَطِيعُونَ

***On the day when the shin will be exposed, and they will be called to bow down, but they will be unable. [al-Qalam 68:42]***

May Allah ﷻ protect us from such a fate. Some individuals, upon experiencing the Divine presence and being called to prostrate, will find themselves unable to do so:

خَاشِعَةً أَبْصَارُهُمْ تَرْهَقُهُمْ ذِلَّةٌ ۖ وَقَدْ كَانُوا يُدْعَوْنَ إِلَى السُّجُودِ وَهُمْ سَالِمُونَ

***Their eyes subdued, covered with shame. They were invited to prostrate when they were sound. [al-Qalam 68:43]***

The Prophet ﷺ taught us that the people of faith will be recognised on the Day of Judgement by the marks of prostration on their foreheads—a testament to their devotion and regular prostration in this life. This physical mark will become a spiritual badge of honour, distinguishing those who habitually prostrated themselves before their Lord from those who rejected this act of submission.

Some individuals might press their foreheads forcefully into the ground or prostrate on particularly rough surfaces, whilst others may naturally develop visible marks on their foreheads from frequent *sujūd*. Whilst this physical mark should not be discredited, one can easily miss the real significance of what the Prophet ﷺ was communicating. Indeed, there are many people who perform abundant prostrations without acquiring these physical traces.

The Prophet ﷺ spoke of spiritual marks—visible to Allah ﷻ and His Angels—that will become prominent on the Day of Judgement. So momentous are these spiritual marks that the Prophet ﷺ said, "The Fire will consume all of the son of Adam ﷺ except the mark of prostration. Allah ﷻ has forbidden the Fire to consume the mark of prostration" (Sunan Ibn Mājah 4326). This refers to those who might endure the Hellfire for a period whilst having performed sincere *sujūd* in the world. They will retain this mark upon their foreheads. The Hellfire itself lacks the power to consume this mark of devotion, provided the prostration was performed purely and sincerely for the sake of Allah ﷻ.

This moving concept is illustrated in the story of Aḥnaf ibn Qays ؓ and his visit to Masjid al-Aqṣā. Upon entering the mosque, he encountered a man deeply immersed in prostration. Intrigued by this display of devotion, he inquired about the number of *rakʿāt* (units of prayer) the man had offered that night. With characteristic humility, the man responded that, whilst he was unsure of the count, Allah ﷻ certainly knew. When Aḥnaf رحمه الله asked about the man's unusually long *sujūd*—something he had never witnessed before—the man, overcome with emotion, shared that the Prophet ﷺ had taught him that each *Sajdah* performed with sincerity elevates one's spiritual rank and expiates a sin.

With each prostration to Allah ﷻ, you ascend by one degree. Simultaneously, one of your sins—those obstacles to spiritual elevation—is removed by the mercy of Allah ﷻ. This profound understanding motivated the man to continue his prostrations throughout the night. Aḥnaf رحمه الله, recognising that he was in the presence of someone special, asked if the man had known the Prophet ﷺ personally. When the man confirmed this, Aḥnaf رحمه الله inquired about his identity. Subḥān Allāh! It was none other than Abū Dharr al-Ghifārī رضي الله عنه.

The significance of finding Abū Dharr رضي الله عنه spending his night in prostration at Masjid al-Aqṣā should not be overlooked. He was known for his concern about materialism infiltrating the ummah, and here he was, elevating himself in the sight of Allah ﷻ through prolonged *sujūd*. This encapsulates the Qurānic description of the *ʿibād al-Raḥmān*:

وَالَّذِينَ يَبِيتُونَ لِرَبِّهِمْ سُجَّدًا وَقِيَامًا

***And those who pass the night before their Lord, prostrating and standing. [al-Furqān 25:64]***

Sahl ibn Saʿd ﷺ reported, "Jibrīl ﷺ came to the Prophet ﷺ and said, 'O Muḥammad ﷺ, live as you wish, for you will surely die. Work as you wish, for you will surely be repaid. Love whomever you wish, for you will surely be separated. Know that the nobility of the believer is in night prayer, and his honour is in his independence on others'" (al-Muʿjam al-Awsaṭ li-l-Ṭabarānī 4278). To truly manifest the qualities of *ʿibād al-Raḥmān* when dealing with others, we must commit to secluded communion with *al-Raḥmān* during the night.

When Imam al-Ḥasan al-Baṣrī ﷺ was asked why the people of *qiyām al-layl*, despite their lack of sleep, possessed the most radiant faces, he explained: "Because they secluded themselves at night with *al-Raḥmān*, and consequently, Allah ﷻ graced them with His Divine light."

Allāhu akbar! We must glorify our Lord ﷻ and strive to be among *al-sājidīn*, those who prostrate themselves before Him. We pray that Allah ﷻ grants us lengthy nights in *qiyām* and *sujūd*, extended periods of standing and prostration in His presence, and a deep connection with Him. May He bestow upon us the type of humility that elevates our status and honour in His sight, allowing us to be concerned solely with His gaze, regardless of who surrounds us.

We beseech Allah to instill in our hearts the sincerity that will guide us through life's journey. Furthermore, we pray that He allows us to depart this world whilst in *sujūd*. Subḥān Allāh! Only a select few are blessed with death in *sujūd*. In moments of prostration, we should earnestly supplicate, "O Allah, let me pass away in this state, let me die whilst in *sujūd*." We will be resurrected in the manner of our death, and the greatest honour on the Day of Judgement will be to be in a state of prostration, following the example of our beloved Prophet. Conversely, the most profound disgrace on that day will befall those who find themselves unable to prostrate.

Therefore, implore Allah, "O Allah, allow me to die in a state of prostration to You. Let that be my termination, yā Rabb al-ʿĀlamīn!" We beseech Allah to transform our *sujūd* into our grand escape from this world, make it our most significant comfort, and bestow upon us the honour it represents. We ask Allah to enable what is generated in the *sujūd* to guide us through the times when we are not in *sujūd*. We plead with Allah to elevate us, as He elevated Rabīʿah ibn Kaʿb al-Aslamī, to the companionship of the Prophet. Allāhumma āmīn.

# Chapter Three Summary

وَالَّذِينَ يَبِيتُونَ لِرَبِّهِمْ سُجَّدًا وَقِيَامًا

*"And those who spend [part of] the night to their Lord prostrating and standing [in prayer]."* (25:64)

## Who is this verse referring to?

Those who spend time in their homes with their Lord.

- The *'Ibād al-Raḥmān* see isolation as an opportunity to **enjoy seclusion with Allah.**
- They energize themselves by spending their nights with Him. To be composed, have a mild presence.

---

## Why does this verse emphasize *sujūd*?

***"The servant is closest to his Lord during prostration, so increase your supplications therein."*** (Sahih Muslim 482)

- It's the closest you can get to your Lord.
- In salah, the entire *rak'ah* is building up to the *Sajdah.*
- *Sajdah* is the act we should be driven to in hardship and in gratitude, in pain and in pleasure.
- The more you lower your body, the higher your soul ascends.

## What are the practical effects of *Sajdah*?

*"And We already know that your breast is constrained by what they say. So exalt [Allah] with praise of your Lord and be of those who prostrate [to Him]." (15:97-98)*

- *Sajdah* has healing powers for those who are distressed.
- The *'Ibād al-Raḥmān* draw strength for the day by spending the night in voluntary *'ibadah*.
- They fight their beds, but the love of Allah sustains them.
- By praying at night (*qiyam*), they find the strength and ability to perform more acts of obedience to Allah during the day, and vice versa.

---

## How will *sujūd* affect us on Judgement Day?

*The Prophet ﷺ said to me, "Ask." I said, "I ask for your companionship in Paradise." He ﷺ said, "Then help me to do it for you by prostrating often." (Sahih Muslim)*

- It's a mark of the greatest honor. On the Day of Judgement you'll be known by the sign of *sujūd* on your forehead.

- The most humiliated one on the Day of Judgement will be the one who neglected or mocked making *Sajdah*—because they never prostrated in this world.
- On the Day of Judgement, the people of *Sajdah* will be known by a mark on their foreheads that will not be consumed, even if they're being cleansed of other sins in the Fire.

## What does *sujūd* look like?

**The ultimate act of humility is falling in tearful prostration to *al-Raḥmān*.**

| ***KHUDU'*** | ***KHUSHU'*** |
| --- | --- |
| The physical act of humbling yourself to Allah | The internal spiritual act of humbling yourself to Allah |
| Prostrating with your forehead connected to the ground in humility | Intently expressing your innermost feelings and love for Allah |
| In *qiyam*, having long moments of *Sajdah* in the depths of the night | In *qiyam*, praising Allah in *Sajdah* straight from the depths of your heart, in your own words |

## What does it look like to be a person of *Sajdah*?

**The *'Ibād al-Raḥmān* who pray *qiyam* and make frequent *Sajdah*...**

...deal with the world by shining peace.

...turn around and express sincere love, even to people who once hurt them.

... respond to others with calm, sincere *sujūd.*

...don't show off their time spent in worship by acting like martyrs.

... recognize that humble ranks are present in every generation.

... prefer *khushu'* over knowledge without humility.

... value inner presence while in *sujūd* over loudness or long recitation.

... have the "freshest faces" because when they are in *Sajdah*, they are face-to-face with *al-Raḥmān*, immersed with His light.

---

## How can we become people of *Sajdah*?

*"You do not make a single prostration except that Allah elevates you by a degree and removes one of your sins."*

*(Ibn Abi Dunya)*

## *THINK*

Commit to seclusion-based *qiyam*, even if it's small. Stop for a moment before *sujūd* and pause to thank Allah for choosing you for this prayer.

## *REFLECT*

*Sajdah* can sustain you through the tides of the day. What do you want to say to Allah in *sujūd* that you gain in no other position?

## *REMEMBER*

There is no way to embody qualities of the *'Ibād al-Raḥmān* without nightly *qiyam* and intimate seclusion at night.

## *ACT*

Cry to Allah often. Connect with Him by complaining to Him—but only to seek His comfort and closeness. Speak to Him softly in prostration, in *qiyam* in your own language.

CHAPTER 4

# Prayer and Protection

وَالَّذِينَ يَقُولُونَ رَبَّنَا اصْرِفْ عَنَّا عَذَابَ جَهَنَّمَ ۖ إِنَّ عَذَابَهَا كَانَ غَرَامًا ۞ إِنَّهَا سَاءَتْ مُسْتَقَرًّا وَمُقَامًا

***And those who say, "Our Lord! Avert the suffering of Hell from us! Its suffering is continuous. It is a miserable residence and destination."***
***[al-Furqān 25:65-66]***

Our discussion of *ʿibād al-Raḥmān* and the attributes of *al-Raḥmān* reveals how different aspects of life interweave. We began our discussion with the external world and how to circumvent its challenges, and we concluded with the necessity of taking solace in the night, where we seek secluded moments with our Lord ﷻ. The nobility of the believer is reflected in their night prayer. But within this sacred space of prostration, what do they say with their forehead on the ground? What supplications do these particular servants offer when they seclude themselves in the corners of their homes, privately calling upon Allah ﷻ?

Allah ﷻ tells us about them:

وَالَّذِينَ يَقُولُونَ رَبَّنَا اصْرِفْ عَنَّا عَذَابَ جَهَنَّمَ ۖ إِنَّ عَذَابَهَا كَانَ غَرَامًا ۝ إِنَّهَا سَاءَتْ مُسْتَقَرًّا وَمُقَامًا

***And those who say, "Our Lord! Avert the suffering of Hell from us! Its suffering is continuous. It is a miserable residence and destination." [al-Furqān 25:65-66]***

Subḥān Allāh! The word "*gharāman*", translated here as "continuous", comes from the same route as "*gharīm*", which can be used to describe a creditor who incessantly pursues you. This type of creditor maintains a constant presence, repeatedly calling, watching, and following you, and their surveillance feels inescapable. They never let you forget or escape the debt you owe. In this supplication, the servants describe "*ʿadhāba Jahannam*" (the punishment of Hellfire) as "*gharāman*", likening it to that relentless creditor who will catch you whenever you try to flee.

This metaphor also has a physical dimension, as witnessed by the Prophet ﷺ. On the night of al-Isrāʾ wa al-Miʿrāj, he saw Mālik ﷺ, the Angel guarding the Hellfire. The appearance of Mālik ﷺ was terrifying, not due to his natural form, but because Allah ﷻ makes him appear frightening to Hell's inhabitants. The guardians of Hellfire prevent any escape—it is *gharāman*, continuously pulling people back.

People attempt to avoid thinking about the punishment of the Hereafter so that they do not feel guilty about their actions. Regarding worldly commitments, some see a convenience in procrastination. Allah ﷻ tells us:

وَقَالُوا لَنْ تَمَسَّنَا النَّارُ إِلَّا أَيَّامًا مَعْدُودَةً ۚ قُلْ
أَتَّخَذْتُمْ عِنْدَ اللَّهِ عَهْدًا فَلَنْ يُخْلِفَ اللَّهُ عَهْدَهُ ۖ أَمْ
تَقُولُونَ عَلَى اللَّهِ مَا لَا تَعْلَمُونَ

***And they say, "The Fire will not touch us except for a number of days." Say, "Have you received a promise from Allah—Allah never breaks His promise—or are you saying about Allah what you do not know?" [al-Baqarah 2:80]***

Some people trivialise sins by thinking that even if they enter Hellfire, it will only be for a few days, and that eventually, *lā ilāha illā Allāh* will deliver them to safety.

This mindset leads to justifications of persisting in sin, indulging in minor transgressions, occasional cheating, and other wrongdoings. Some may begin to underestimate the consequences of their actions. However, the *rajulun gharīm* is a stalker to whom you are indebted and who will tirelessly pursue you until they have retrieved what is rightfully theirs. This is how Hellfire is depicted; its punishment is interminable.

The phrase "*innahā sā'at mustaqarran wa muqāman*" denotes a dreadful dwelling and resting place. "*Sā'at mustaqarran*" refers to an "eternal location", whilst "*muqāman*", from the same root as "*iqāmah*", signifies "endless duration". "*Mustaqarran*" indicates an eternal location, whilst "*muqāman*" suggests infinite punishment. Together, the two descriptions capture these servants' gripping fear of Hellfire's torment.

The *ʿibād al-Raḥmān* pray for salvation. Imam al-Qurṭubī makes a compelling observation about their certainty—they speak as if they have witnessed Hellfire, which points to their deep conviction in its existence.

وَالَّذِينَ يَقُولُونَ رَبَّنَا اصْرِفْ عَنَّا عَذَابَ جَهَنَّمَ ۖ إِنَّ
عَذَابَهَا كَانَ غَرَامًا ۝ إِنَّهَا سَاءَتْ مُسْتَقَرًّا وَمُقَامًا

***And those who say, "Our Lord! Avert the suffering of Hell from us! Its suffering is continuous. It is a miserable residence and destination." [al-Furqān 25:65-66]***

They speak with conviction and with knowledge, as if they had witnessed it themselves. Their sureness about its existence and punishment is complete; nothing is hypothetical.

This certainty requires no direct or physical experience because those who believe in the Unseen "*alladhīna yu'minūna bi al-ghayb*" accept it as a tenet of their faith. When Allah ﷻ informs us of something through *al-ṣādiq al-maṣdūq*, the trustworthy Prophet ﷺ, it becomes as if we have seen it ourselves. ʿAlī ibn Abī Ṭālib ؓ once declared that even if he were to see Paradise with his own eyes, his desire for it would not increase, nor would seeing Hellfire increase his fear of it, such was his certainty in their existence—*al-jannatu ḥaqqun wa al-nāru ḥaqqun* (Heaven is certain and Hellfire is certain).

This theme of certainty appears in the ḥadīth about Angels discovering circles of *dhikr*. When Allah ﷻ asks the Angels what these people hope for, they respond: Paradise. Though they have not seen it, their expression of desire suggests they have. Allah ﷻ then asks the Angels to imagine how much more they would desire it upon seeing it. As for the Hellfire, even without witnessing it, their fear is intense—how much more would they fear it if they had seen it with their own eyes?

If they had seen it, they would progress from *ʿilm al-yaqīn* (certain knowledge) to *ʿayn al yaqīn* (certainty of direct experience). As a person moves between these two levels, the understanding they attain becomes as certain as if they had witnessed the thing directly. This heightened certainty draws one closer to Allah ﷻ and inspires righteous actions.

One of the *salaf*, Abū Ḥazm ؒ, reflected one night

on those who were missing out on *qiyām al-layl*, saying, "I marvel at Paradise—how can its seeker sleep?" He expressed equal amazement regarding the Hellfire, wondering how someone trying to escape it could find rest. As Allah ﷻ mentions in Sūrah al-Sajdah, these servants call upon their Lord out of both fear and hope. This simultaneous yearning for Paradise and dread of Hellfire naturally reduces sleep, leading to more night prayer, increased seclusion, and fervent supplications seeking the protection and elevation of Allah ﷻ.

Yet the ultimate aspiration transcends both fear and hope, reaching a state where the desire of the pleasure of Allah ﷻ becomes one's primary motivator. 'Umar ibn al-Khaṭṭāb ؓ spoke of Ṣuhayb al-Rūmī ؓ, saying, "Even if he did not fear Allah ﷻ, he would still not disobey Him." Why? Because his love for Allah ﷻ had reached such heights—he would not disobey someone he loved so intensely. This aligns with the metaphor offered by Ibn al-Qayyim ؒ: the body of the believer is the love of Allah ﷻ, whilst fear and hope serve as its two wings. Note that whenever we mention fear in this regard, we are specifically referring to a healthy, galvanising fear, not despair. This galvanising fear should never lead to hopelessness, just as a galvanising hope should never lead to delusion.

Recall the *āyāt* we are studying:

وَعِبَادُ الرَّحْمَٰنِ الَّذِينَ يَمْشُونَ عَلَى الْأَرْضِ
هَوْنًا وَإِذَا خَاطَبَهُمُ الْجَاهِلُونَ قَالُوا سَلَامًا ۞ وَالَّذِينَ
يَبِيتُونَ لِرَبِّهِمْ سُجَّدًا وَقِيَامًا ۞ وَالَّذِينَ يَقُولُونَ رَبَّنَا
اصْرِفْ عَنَّا عَذَابَ جَهَنَّمَ ۖ إِنَّ عَذَابَهَا كَانَ غَرَامًا ۞
إِنَّهَا سَاءَتْ مُسْتَقَرًّا وَمُقَامًا

***The servants of the Most Merciful are those who walk on the earth modestly, and when the ignorant address them, they say, "Peace." And those who pass the night before their Lord, prostrating and standing. And those who say, "Our Lord! Avert the suffering of Hell from us! Its suffering is continuous. It is a miserable residence and destination." [al-Furqān 25:63-66]***

Connections between the verses begin to emerge. Firstly, these individuals are *ʿibād al-Raḥmān*, servants of the Most Merciful, who beseech Allah ﷻ for His mercy. There is an inherent beauty in this. Secondly, a grave danger ominously lurks, and it can harm those who stray from living a righteous life, both in private and public.

The *ʿibād al-Raḥmān* are described thus far as those who pray at night "*yabītūna li-rabbihim sujjadan wa qiyāman*" whilst displaying exceptional grace in their daily interactions with the creation of Allah ﷻ. They faithfully express gratitude through nightly prayer and supplication, establishing a compelling connection between their private and public lives.

Being so fervent, it is possible that they could develop an attitude of pride and conceit or view themselves in an inflated light. This could lead to boastfulness, arrogance, judgemental attitudes, or even dismissing the threat of Hellfire as something only of concern to others.

It is crucial to understand that if Shayṭān cannot attack from one path, he will attempt another. If unable to tempt a person into sins—whether through personal desires or responding to foolishness—he will try to corrupt them through prayer, fasting, and other virtuous deeds, infusing them with pride and ostentation.

The *ʿibād al-Raḥmān* understand this and do not become presumptuous. They do not consider themselves to be automatically counted amongst the beloved of Allah ﷻ and therefore exempt from worry. They do not arrogantly assume that the Hellfire—which one might view as being reserved for the foolish or those who do not pray at night like they do—will not touch them. They avoid placing themselves above others who might be engaged in worldly activities whilst they pray. Despite their virtuous qualities, fear remains—not a crippling fear, but a healthy awareness that keeps them humble and sincere in their devotion.

The servants of the Most Merciful maintain such a profound fear of Allah ﷻ that they continuously beseech Him for salvation from Hellfire's punishment. This connects to the previous verse, in which we are told:

وَإِذَا خَاطَبَهُمُ الْجَاهِلُونَ قَالُوا سَلَامًا

***And when the ignorant address them, they say, "Peace." [al-Furqān 25:63]***

The *ʿibād al-Raḥmān* always remain focused, despite others' attempts to distract them. Consider someone rushing to make a crucial appointment. As they hurry towards their destination, various incidents occur along the way. Nevertheless, their singular focus remains reaching their goal. Imagine arriving at the parking lot at 1:59 p.m for a 2:00 p.m appointment—as you sprint toward your destination, someone hurls an insult or makes a senseless comment. You disregard it entirely, for your mind is fixed on reaching your appointment. Similarly, *ʿibād al-Raḥmān* are so deeply immersed in contemplating the gravity of the Hereafter that worldly trivialities find no room in their consciousness. They are too preoccupied with the Hereafter's severity to entertain this world's frivolities. Consequently, they cannot afford to concern themselves with petty insults or those who target their reputation. Petty disputes and saving one's face from insults pale in comparison to protecting one's face from the Hellfire on the Day of Judgement—there simply is no time for anything else.

The severity of *ʿadhāb al-ākhirah* (the punishment of the Hereafter) far outweighs any worldly suffering. Consider the story of ʿUthmān ؓ who, in his eighties, once pinched a young boy's ear and felt immediate remorse. He implored the youth to reciprocate, but the boy hesitated, recognising the elevated status of ʿUthmān ؓ, a man whom the Prophet ﷺ revered and the Angels respected. Despite his insistence, the boy refused to hit ʿUthmān ؓ back, acknowledging him as the khalīfah and the noblest man alive. ʿUthmān ؓ persisted, explaining that this world's consequences are nothing compared to the Hereafter's. He preferred enduring a minor injury now to facing severe repurcussions in the life to come.

Prioritising the Hereafter is further illuminated in a ḥadīth from ʿĀʾishah ؓ, who said, "I heard the Messenger of Allah ﷺ saying, 'The people will be assembled on the Day of Resurrection barefooted, naked and uncircumcised.' I said, "O Messenger of Allah! Will the men and the women be together on that Day, looking at one another?" The Messenger of Allah

ﷺ replied, ‘O ʿĀʾishah, the situation will be too grave for that’” (Riyāḍ al-Ṣāliḥīn 411).

The matter is indeed too grave for that, and the *ʿibād al-Raḥmān* are aware of this fact. This keeps them focused on what truly matters, rather than becoming ensnared in worldly obsessions.

We must reflect on how much importance we assign to maintaining certain features of this life. Whenever these aspects show flaws, our equilibrium shatters. Instead, anchor yourself to the Hereafter, for it alone remains certain. Pursue the pleasure of Allah ﷻ, for this has proven to be a worthier goal. When the world presents its inevitable challenges, your primary objective and path remain intact if you stay connected to these truths.

The Qurʾān repeatedly emphasises the connection between urgency and awareness. Allah ﷻ reveals Himself in two ways until the truth becomes clear: through signs in the horizons and within ourselves. Allah ﷻ says:

وَفِي الْأَرْضِ آيَاتٌ لِّلْمُوقِنِينَ ۞ وَفِي
أَنفُسِكُمْ ۚ أَفَلَا تُبْصِرُونَ ۞ وَفِي السَّمَاءِ رِزْقُكُمْ
وَمَا تُوعَدُونَ ۞ فَوَرَبِّ السَّمَاءِ وَالْأَرْضِ إِنَّهُ
لَحَقٌّ مِّثْلَ مَا أَنَّكُمْ تَنطِقُونَ

***And in the earth are signs for the assured. And in yourselves—do you still not see? And in the Heavens is your provision and what you have been oathed. Then by the Lord of the Heavens and the earth, certainly it is the truth just as you speak among yourselves.* *[al-Dhāriyāt 51:20-23]***

In Sūrah Āl ʿImrān, Allah ﷻ mentions those who contemplate creation, saying:

الَّذِينَ يَذْكُرُونَ اللَّهَ قِيَامًا وَقُعُودًا وَعَلَىٰ جُنُوبِهِمْ وَيَتَفَكَّرُونَ فِي خَلْقِ السَّمَاوَاتِ وَالْأَرْضِ رَبَّنَا مَا خَلَقْتَ هَٰذَا بَاطِلًا سُبْحَانَكَ فَقِنَا عَذَابَ النَّارِ

***Those who remember Allah whilst standing, sitting, and on their sides; and they reflect upon the creation of the Heavens and the earth: "Our Lord, You did not create this in vain. Glory be to You! So protect us from the suffering of the Fire." [Āl ʿImrān 3:191]***

Those who observe the horizons and all the creations of Allah ﷻ—the stars, moon, sun, grass, flowers, mountains, and water—arrive at this momentous realisation: "Our Lord, You did not create this in vain." This awareness, born from contemplating creation, leads them first to declare the perfection of Allah ﷻ and then to seek protection from the Fire. Why? Because genuine awareness generates spiritual urgency.

This urgency manifests in their actions:

وَالَّذِينَ يَبِيتُونَ لِرَبِّهِمْ سُجَّدًا وَقِيَامًا

***And those who pass the night before their Lord, prostrating and standing.* [al-Furqān 25:64]**

It manifests when a person retreats to the corner of their home for prostration and prayer. But where does this awareness originate? It stems from the recognition of our own selves, creation, and actions. This self-awareness leads to the urgent supplication, "O Allah ﷻ, protect us from the Fire. O Allah ﷻ, shield us from the punishment."

In our spiritual journey, both fear and hope serve a purpose. *Khawf* (fear) protects us from *nifāq* (hypocrisy) in a way that hope cannot. Meanwhile, *ṭamaʿ* (hope) shields us from *shahawāt* (base desires), because it teaches us to yearn for something greater; elevating our wish for Paradise and the pleasure of Allah ﷻ above our immediate worldly desires. These two elements of spiritual cultivation are distinct yet equally crucial. Allah ﷻ says:

تَتَجَافَىٰ جُنُوبُهُمْ عَنِ الْمَضَاجِعِ يَدْعُونَ رَبَّهُمْ خَوْفًا وَطَمَعًا وَمِمَّا رَزَقْنَاهُمْ يُنْفِقُونَ

***Their sides shun their beds, as they pray to their Lord, out of reverence and hope; and from Our provisions to them, they give. [al-Sajdah 32:16]***

The necessity of fear in protecting against hypocrisy becomes evident in the question ʿĀʾishah ﵂ asked the Prophet ﷺ about the *āyah* in Sūrah al-Muʾminūn:

أُولَٰئِكَ يُسَارِعُونَ فِي الْخَيْرَاتِ وَهُمْ لَهَا سَابِقُونَ

***It is they who race towards good deeds, and they will reach them first. [al-Muʾminūn 23:61]***

She asked, "'Is this the one who commits adultery, steals and drinks alcohol?' The Prophet ﷺ replied, "No, O daughter of Abū Bakr [or O daughter of al-Ṣiddīq (the truthful)], rather it is a man who fasts and gives charity and prays, but he fears that they will not be accepted from him"'" (Sunan Ibn Mājah 4198).

Incidentally, the Prophet ﷺ referring to ʿĀʾishah ﵂ as "daughter of the truthful" (Bint al-Ṣiddīq) is thought to be an acknowledgement of her sincerity and honesty. There is much to learn from his mannerisms at home with his wives, as well as their conduct with him.

Her question arose from her observing those who, upon repenting to Allah ﷻ, rush to transform their lives. They often appear overzealous, attempting to compensate for extreme sin with extreme deeds. Whilst commendable, this approach runs the risk of potential burnout or relapse. Unfortunately, this is a common pattern—someone commits a grave sin, repents, sets unrealistic expectations, faces disappointment, and then returns to their past ways.

'Ā'ishah ﵂ witnessed the opposite among the Ṣaḥābah, a community of converts that included the likes of 'Umar ibn al-Khaṭṭāb ﵁. They experienced dramatic transformations but managed to stay upright once guided. We can study the examples of 'Umar and Ḥamzah ﵄ before and after embracing Islam. They remained free from pride and conceit, never becoming complacent or thinking, "I perform all these virtuous acts, so I must be righteous."

Such complacency represents a dangerous spiritual disease. It is particularly insidious because it is harder to detect than obvious sins. When immersed in sin, a person can more easily acknowledge their transgression. But when engaged in good deeds whilst simultaneously developing pride, conceit, or self-righteousness, these spiritual flaws become almost invisible.

This is why the Prophet ﷺ warned, "If you did not sin, I would fear for you something worse than that: conceit, conceit" (Ṣaḥīḥ al-Jāmiʿ 5303). This sense of pride can lead to belittling others and looking down upon them, a spiritual ailment that Ibn al-Qayyim  explored in detail.

Ibn al-Qayyim  noted that to sleep through the night and awaken filled with *nādima* (regret) was superior to spending an entire night in *qiyām al-layl*, only to rise in the morning filled with pride, because the one who experiences regret kindles their yearning to draw closer to Allah . Despite their shortcomings, they maintain their spiritual striving. Conversely, the one who spends the entire night in prayer but falls prey to self-aggrandizement has fallen from grace.

This point becomes particularly crucial for those who are newly practising and might lose sight of their own past and begin to disdain others. The Qurʾān provides us with a remedy:

وَإِذَا خَاطَبَهُمُ الْجَاهِلُونَ قَالُوا سَلَامًا

***And when the ignorant address them, they say, "Peace." [al-Furqān 25:63]***

This demonstrates a connection between their humble response to foolish detractors and their recognition of potential goodness in even the most seemingly wayward individual.

The *salaf* understood that, through some hidden virtue known only to Allah ﷻ, a person who was known to be a transgressor might ultimately prove superior to someone considered to be a scholar. The visible sinner, despite their reputation, may have performed a righteous deed that will secure their salvation and entry into Paradise. Meanwhile, one known for piety and religious observance might harbour no such safety net.

Our pious predecessors never looked down upon those openly committing sins. Their awareness of their own shortcomings remained acute, and the fear of their own flaws remained tangible. They always considered the possibility of some hidden good in the sinner, acknowledging that the sinner might avoid certain sins that they themselves commit, potentially making them more virtuous in the sight of Allah ﷻ.

Ḥudhayfah ibn al-Yamān ﵁ was a shining example of this mindset. Whilst several Ṣaḥābah asked the Prophet ﷺ about good deeds and how to attain reward, Ḥudhayfah ﵁ inquired about evil deeds and how to avoid them. This vigilance earned him the trust of the Prophet ﷺ, who knew Ḥudhayfah ﵁ would be protected from hypocrisy. Later on, Ḥudhayfah ﵁ was the person the Prophet ﷺ secretly told the names of the Hypocrites.

ʿUmar ibn al-Khaṭṭāb, despite being among those guaranteed Paradise, once asked Ḥudhayfah if his name was amongst the Hypocrites the Prophet had mentioned. His extended nights of *qiyām* and *khidmah* did not breed pride or haughtiness. Instead, they deepened his humility and consciousness of needing the protection of Allah.

Our supplications should include both requests for protection from the terrors of Jahannam and requests for elevation in Jannah. The Prophet said, "For whoever asks Allah for Paradise three times, Paradise says, 'O Allah, admit him into Paradise,' and for whoever seeks refuge from the Fire three times, the Fire says, 'O Allah, save him from the Fire'" (Jāmiʿ al-Tirmidhī 2572).

May Allah instill in us an acute awareness of the Hereafter and protect us from the punishments of the grave and the Fire, replacing it with the bounties of Paradise and the companionship of His Messenger. May Allah make us people who balance our love for Him, hope in Him, and fear of Him. May these qualities guide us back to Him, so that we might be counted among *ʿibād al-Raḥmān*, the servants of the Most Merciful. Allāhumma āmīn.

# Chapter Four Summary

رَبَّنَا ٱصْرِفْ عَنَّا عَذَابَ جَهَنَّمَ إِنَّ عَذَابَهَا
كَانَ غَرَامًا إِنَّهَا سَآءَتْ مُسْتَقَرًّا وَمُقَامًا

*"Our Lord, avert from us the punishment of Hell. Indeed, its punishment is ever adhering. Indeed, it is evil as a settlement and residence." (25:64)*

## What do those who spend their nights in prayer ask for?

Those who spend their time in their homes with their Lord:

- They ask for protection from the Fire.
- Their requests are passionate and urgent.
- They have complete certainty of the Fire and the ability of Allah to save us from it.

## Why is this the topic of their *qiyam*?

*"They arise from [their] beds; they supplicate to their Lord in fear and hope..." (32:16)*

- The *'Ibād al-Raḥmān* are appealing to Allah for His *raḥmah*.
- Their prayers are motivated by an awareness of the Hereafter and an urgency to earn Allah's pleasure.
- Hell is described in the above verses as:

- *Gharāma*: something that stalks you, from which you can't escape.
- *Mustaqarr*: an ever-present place.
- *Muqām*: lasting for a never-ending period of time.

- It is only through the intercession of Allah that we are rescued from punishment.
- Allah asks us to call out to Him with a healthy dose of both fear and hope.

## What does healthy fear and hope in Allah look like?

The goal of worship is to get to the point where fear and hope are overcome by love of Allah's pleasure.

| ***HEALTHY FEAR (KHAWF)*** | ***HEALTHY HOPE (TAMA')*** |
|---|---|
| Being aware of consequences, but never despairing in Allah's mercy | Being aware of Allah's *raḥmah*, but never being deluded by it |
| Purpose is to balance out blind hope | Purpose is to balance out blind fear |
| Protects from hypocrisy (*nifaq*) that comes from arrogance | Protects from desires (*shahawat*) that come from heedlessness |

## Can righteousness make you more susceptible to arrogance?

*"If you were not to sin, I would fear for you something greater than sin: that you would become conceited." [Sahih Al-Jami' 5303]*

Righteous acts can lead to arrogance if not performed mindfully.

- If Shayṭān can't get you to commit sins or treat people badly, he'll push you to believe you're better than others.
- To develop self-righteousness is worse than sinning. It's easier to recognize your shortcomings from a place of sin.

## How do you avoid arrogance?

*"For you to sleep all night and wake up in regret is better than for you to spend the whole night in qiyam and wake up in the morning with pride." [Ibn Al-Qayyim]*

- Remember that even when we may have good qualities, we are also sinners.
- The successful are those who do good but always strive to do more without feeding the self.

- Cultivate a healthy fear for your own fate while not despairing in Allah's mercy.

  - The *'Ibād al-Raḥmān* are too busy worrying about the severity of the Hereafter to be thinking about the pettiness of this world.

- Learn from the way our pious predecessors viewed the world:

  - 'The sinner may have some deed that will enter them into Paradise, while the worshipper may have a fatal sin that will lead them astray.'

---

## How can we develop a healthy balance of fear and hope in *qiyam*?

*"Whoever asks Allah for Heaven three times, Heaven responds, 'Oh Allah, enter them into Paradise.' Whoever asks Allah for protection from Hell three times, Hell responds, 'Oh Allah, protect them from me.'" [Sunan at-Tirmidhi 2572]*

*THINK*

What is your qiyam like?

Do you have in your sights the reality of the Hereafter or are you preoccupied with this world?

---

*REFLECT*

When you belittle a sin, you belittle the consequences of that sin. How can you recognize your sins and allow them to keep your arrogance in check?

---

*REMEMBER*

To call out to Allah with a balance of fear, hope, and love means less sleep and more prayer, seclusion and *du'ā*.

---

*ACT*

Ask for protection from the Fire with urgency, as if you can see it. Ask for entrance into Paradise with hope, as if you can see it. Tie yourself to the Afterlife and to Allah, because those are certain, while this life is not.

# CHAPTER 5

# Generosity and Moderation

وَالَّذِينَ إِذَا أَنْفَقُوا لَمْ يُسْرِفُوا وَلَمْ
يَقْتُرُوا وَكَانَ بَيْنَ ذَٰلِكَ قَوَامًا

***And those who, when they spend, are neither wasteful nor stingy, but choose a course in between.***
***[al-Furqān 25:67]***

Allah ﷾ continues in His description of the servants of the Most Merciful in the next *āyah*. They are those who spend neither extravagantly, nor are they miserly. Instead, they are moderate and in equilibrium. Allah ﷾ defines the middle ground by highlighting the two extremities. This provides an opportunity for reflection—where do the boundaries of extravagance and miserliness end, and how relative are these terms? These are questions we will soon unpack. The core principle to remember, however, is that *ʿibād al-Raḥmān* have healthy spending habits.

Often, when we think about spirituality, we focus on overt acts of worship and asceticism. However, Allah ﷾ is showing us that there is more to think about. The focus in this *āyah* is not on charity, but on how one manages their personal finances.

The Prophet ﷺ said, "It is [part of] a man's wisdom to adhere to the middle path in spending" (Maʿārif al-Qur'ān). He also said, "The person who sticks to the middle path and moderation in spending will never become destitute or poor" (Maʿārif al-Qur'ān). Healthy spending habits are thus a sign of intelligence and discernment.

Why would the Prophet ﷺ specifically refer to this approach to finances as being wise? In Arabic, *ḥikmah* (wisdom) implies governance or control, analogous to a horse's reins. If knowledge (*ʿilm*) represents the horse, *ḥikmah* represents the ability to guide and apply that knowledge appropriately. *Ḥikmah* also denotes authority. Therefore, when the Prophet ﷺ labels this balance as *ḥikmah*, he suggests that such individuals possess sound understanding of balance and order, preventing matters from spiraling out of control—something particularly crucial in spending, where people often abandon restraint.

Many recent studies have shown that a person's spending habits are intrinsically linked to their character. People with poor spending habits frequently display poor control in other areas of their lives. The *āyah* mentioned above links fiscal discipline with spiritual excellence in a manner most of us do not appreciate.

A common piece of financial advice young adults

receive is that they should learn to live on a budget—but what does this mean from an Islamic perspective? The connection is in the skill of restraint. Not overspending is a form of resisting temptation. Elsewhere in the Qurʾān, Allah ﷻ says:

وَابْتَغِ فِيمَا آتَاكَ اللَّهُ الدَّارَ الْآخِرَةَ ۖ وَلَا تَنسَ نَصِيبَكَ مِنَ الدُّنْيَا ۖ وَأَحْسِن كَمَا أَحْسَنَ اللَّهُ إِلَيْكَ ۖ وَلَا تَبْغِ الْفَسَادَ فِي الْأَرْضِ ۖ إِنَّ اللَّهَ لَا يُحِبُّ الْمُفْسِدِينَ

***But seek, with what Allah has given you, the Home of the Hereafter. And do not neglect your share of this world. And be charitable, as Allah is charitable to you. And do not work corruption on earth—Allah does not like the corruptors."* [al-Qaṣaṣ 28:77]**

This *āyah* reminds us not to be negligent in worldly affairs but to also avoid extravagance. Living within a budget essentially means restraining desires and limiting worldly consumption. These are important skills for every Muslim to develop.

Another crucial aspect of healthy spending involves avoiding impulsive purchases. In our era of instant gratification, where delivery services offer immediate satisfaction with a single button press, the temptation for impulsive buying grows stronger. The SARS CoV-2 pandemic has only accelerated this trend towards convenient online shopping. Regardless of financial status, the urge to buy impulsively affects everyone.

This is intrinsically linked to patience. The Prophet ﷺ taught us, "Deliberateness is from Allah ﷻ and haste is from Shayṭān" (Jāmiʿ al-Tirmidhī 2012). Our haste, manifesting in impulsive behaviours—whether in a shopping mall or during an argument at home—represents a significant spiritual flaw. Impulsivity ranks among the worst qualities one can possess, as it is something Shayṭān actively encourages. His strategy involves rushing us into mistakes and then convincing us that we cannot escape their consequences, promoting reckless behaviour in all areas of life. When you act impulsively, you do not consider your actions beforehand. Subsequently, after you act, Shayṭān convinces you that there is no point in trying to return to Allah ﷻ—you have already faltered, so you might as well continue on that path.

Researching products before purchase is also crucial. A person should not impulsively buy something simply because it is aesthetically pleasing, but should undertake thorough research beforehand. After all, the Prophet ﷺ instructed us to avoid *al-Shubuhāt* (doubtful matters).

Subḥān Allāh! As Ibn Zaymiyya ﷺ expressed, there are two elements that undermine a person's spirituality: indulgence in *shahawāt* (desires) and *shubuhāt* (doubtful matters). Indeed, either can spiritually sink a person.

The Prophet ﷺ advised us to exercise caution when it comes to doubtful matters due to the potential impact on our spirituality. This advice is echoed today by numerous financial self-help gurus who encourage prudent spending—learn to research products before buying, allow them some time on the market, observe people's interactions with them, and consider the reviews. Currently, however, people tend to pre-order items without conducting any research. They know the next version of a product is about to be released and are eager to secure their order quickly.

The principle of researching before purchasing directly connects to the spiritual practice of avoiding doubtful matters. Abū Ḥanīfah ﷺ brilliantly illustrates this connection. His pioneering approach to *fiqh* made him a towering figure upon whom many depended for guidance. Yet Abū Ḥanīfah ﷺ was not only a scholar, he was also an accomplished merchant. His success in trade did not stem from inherited wealth or the garments he sold, but from his exceptional ability to identify defects that others missed. This skill protected him from being deceived by cloth that appeared to be of high quality at first glance but revealed defects when scrutinised. He meticulously examined areas that others overlooked, like garment edges, and the same thoroughness in commerce was mirrored in his scholarship.

Another tenet of modern financial advice is to avoid spending triggers. Similarly, the Prophet ﷺ taught us not only to avoid sin, but also its precursors—a concept also found in the Qurʾān:

يَا أَيُّهَا النَّاسُ كُلُوا مِمَّا فِي الْأَرْضِ حَلَالًا طَيِّبًا وَلَا تَتَّبِعُوا خُطُوَاتِ الشَّيْطَانِ ۚ إِنَّهُ لَكُمْ عَدُوٌّ مُبِينٌ

***O people! Eat of what is lawful and good on the earth, and do not follow the footsteps of Shayṭān. He is to you an open enemy. [al-Baqarah 2:168]***

We must be mindful of environments that lead to excessive spending. Likewise, we must be mindful of settings that lead to other sins. An example of this is avoiding *khalwah* (seclusion) with unrelated persons from the opposite gender.

Self-study is essential in identifying the things that lead one to sin. Imam al-Ghazālī ؒ in the *Iḥyāʾ*, Ibn al-Jawzī ؒ in *Minhāj al-Qāṣidīn*, and Ibn al-Qayyim ؒ in his *Maqāṣid* all emphasise that true repentance requires identifying and avoiding the triggers of sin. Ibn al-Jawzī ؒ suggests that if your garment snags whilst walking, you should return to the point of entanglement rather than risk tearing it—he uses this as a metaphor to emphasise the importance of tracing your steps back to what led to sin and fixing the issue at its roots.

Anotherr financial principle that is echoed in our religion is exercising gratitude in order to avoid feelings of deprivation or exclusion. Often, people make purchases because they feel left out and are seeing others attain things they do not possess themselves, which leads to dissatisfaction with their own belongings. However, gratitude transforms this perspective. Allah ﷻ declares:

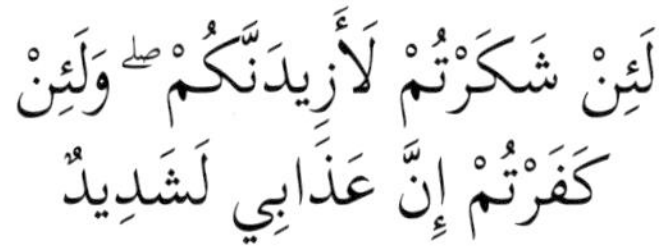

***If you give thanks, I will give you more; but if you are ungrateful, My punishment is severe.***
***[Ibrāhīm 14:7]***

Through gratitude, a person learns to appreciate their existing possessions, reducing their anxiety about unfulfilled desires. There is a direct correlation between *isrāf* (excessive consumption) and the constant pursuit of fulfillment through the acquiring of new products. Those fearing they might miss out or fall behind as others obtain new things can overcome this through gratitude for what they already have.

Subḥān Allāh! These fundamental financial principles, upon careful examination, correlate directly with sound spending habits, one of the qualities of the *ʿibād al-Raḥmān*. But how does Islam define extravagance? Allah ﷻ doesn't explicitly quantify extravagance or stinginess in this passage, leaving much to individual judgement. As with the concepts of good spending habits or appropriate leisure expenditure, the answer varies according to person and circumstance. It is not appropriate to name a specific figure, for people and societies differ. The ancient Arabs had completely different expenses and needs to modern Americans, for example.

So how does Islam view *isrāf* and *tabdhīr*—different levels of extravagance? The *ʿulamāʾ* identify clear features of *isrāf*. Firstly, they assert that spending any amount, even a single dollar, in unlawful ways constitutes *isrāf*. This represents extravagance of the self.

Allah ﷻ says:

قُلْ يَا عِبَادِيَ الَّذِينَ أَسْرَفُوا عَلَىٰ أَنفُسِهِمْ
لَا تَقْنَطُوا مِن رَّحْمَةِ اللَّهِ ۚ إِنَّ اللَّهَ يَغْفِرُ الذُّنُوبَ
جَمِيعًا ۚ إِنَّهُ هُوَ الْغَفُورُ الرَّحِيمُ

***Say, "O My servants who have transgressed against their souls: do not despair of the mercy of Allah, for Allah forgives all sins. He is the Forgiving, the Merciful." [al-Zumar 39:53]***

The scholars interpret extravagance as encompassing any expenditure on prohibited things, regardless of the amount. Living beyond one's means, even with permissible things, is also classified as extravagance—a trap into which many unfortunately stumble. The sunnah of the Prophet ﷺ is to live within one's means. Thus, purchasing items one cannot afford is inadvisable. Whilst such purchases would not be extravagant for someone who can afford them without incurring debt or compromising their religious (e.g., ḥajj) or familial obligations, they are for those who cannot.

Scholars also identify a third type of extravagance: spending money in righteous ways not for the sake of Allah ﷻ, but for public display. This includes purchasing clothes or cars, or hosting ostentatious weddings for show. Unfortunately, extravagant weddings are one of the most common forms of excess within our community today.

*Isrāf* is inextricably linked to how we wish to be perceived by others. A person who indulges in *ḥalāl* to an excessive degree does so to project a certain image. Scholars then pose a more intricate question: what is the ruling for someone who gives *ṣadaqah*, a noble act, but with ill intentions of showing off? This person is using something meant for the sake of Allah ﷻ to achieve the same goal as those who flaunt lavish weddings and fancy cars. Such a person seeks to shape others' perception rather than earn the pleasure of Allah ﷻ. It becomes even more egregious when one uses *ṣadaqah*, a noble form of spending, not for the sake of Allah ﷻ but for personal gain. May Allah ﷻ protect us from such behaviour.

Let us examine the middle ground between miserliness and extravagance in more detail. In Sūrah al-Isrā', Allah ﷻ says:

وَلَا تَجْعَلْ يَدَكَ مَغْلُولَةً إِلَىٰ عُنُقِكَ وَلَا
تَبْسُطْهَا كُلَّ الْبَسْطِ فَتَقْعُدَ مَلُومًا مَحْسُورًا

***And do not keep your hand tied to your neck, nor spread it out entirely, lest you end up liable and regretful.* [al-Isrā' 17:29]**

Allah ﷻ provides analogies for stinginess and wastefulness, and He warns against both extremes.

In Sūrah al-Isrā', Allah ﷻ also says:

وَآتِ ذَا الْقُرْبَىٰ حَقَّهُ وَالْمِسْكِينَ وَابْنَ السَّبِيلِ
وَلَا تُبَذِّرْ تَبْذِيرًا ۞ إِنَّ الْمُبَذِّرِينَ كَانُوا إِخْوَانَ
الشَّيَاطِينِ ۖ وَكَانَ الشَّيْطَانُ لِرَبِّهِ كَفُورًا

***And give the relative his rights, and the poor, and the wayfarer. And do not squander wastefully. The extravagant are brethren of the devils, and Shayṭān is ever ungrateful to his Lord. [al-Isrā' 17:26-27]***

Beginning with family ensures the fulfillment of their rights upon you. This then extends to "*al-miskīn*" (the destitute) and "*ibn al-sabīl*" (literally 'son of the road,' referring to wayfarers and the homeless). Scholars note that when *miskīn* and *ibn al-sabīl* appear together, like islām and *īmān*, their meanings shift. Just as islām represents an external expression of faith and *īmān* represents internal faith when the terms are used together, *miskīn* refers to local poor people—neighbours or community members struggling with bills—whilst *ibn al-sabīl* refers to travellers passing through. Allah ﷻ advises prioritising one's relatives first, then the needy in one's locality, and then those passing through.

*Isrāf* and *tabdhīr* are often translated into English in a similar way, but there is an important distinction between the two. *Isrāf* typically denotes extravagance with permissible matters. It is not used when something forbidden is being purchased, but when something permissible is being over-indulged in. It refers to buying or spending on permissible things either beyond one's means or stretching the boundaries of permissibility until they become questionable. You might overextend your resources or push the limits of what is permissible until it crosses the line into impermissibility.

Conversely, *tabdhīr* refers exclusively to wasteful spending on impermissible things. In the passage quoted above, Allah ﷻ told us that "*al-mubadhdhirīn*" (the wasteful) are "brothers of the devils". What is the connection? Allah ﷻ tells us that Shayṭān was ungrateful to his Lord. Shayṭān used the blessings of Allah ﷻ to disobey Him. This is exactly what someone who spends his wealth on impermissible things does—he uses the blessing of wealth to disobey Allah ﷻ. Thus, employing these blessings in acts of disobedience makes one comparable to Shayṭān himself.

This is the precise mechanism by which one transitions from being a brother or sister in faith to becoming a sibling of devils. Just as Shayṭān exploited the power, position, and prominence that Allah ﷻ bestowed upon him to commit acts of disobedience, spending what you have earned on things that Allah ﷻ has prohibited represents the height of ingratitude.

This encapsulates the distinction between *isrāf* and *tabdhīr*. To reiterate, most scholars state that *isrāf* refers to over-indulgence in permissible things whereas *tabdhīr* is solely related to spending on things that are impermissible.

How, then, does one purify their spending habits? Firstly, give your relatives their due rights. Allah ﷻ reprimands stinginess with the same intensity as He does extravagance. Allah ﷻ does not condemn extravagance and then qualify stinginess as a lesser evil, and depriving those who have a right over you carries the same weight of transgression.

The greatest reward from spending lies in providing for one's family. If you are to be counted amongst the *ʿibād al-Raḥmān*, the primary recipients of your mercy should be your family. What purpose is there in showing mercy to the foolish but being cruel to one's family? We discussed dealing with the *jāhilūn*, those external individuals who are rough and rude, but they hold no right over you. They are merely obstacles on your path back to Allah ﷻ.

However, your family does not constitute an obstacle. It is not appropriate to simply say "*salām*" to your family following every argument, treating them with indifference. Your family are an essential component for progression along a spiritual path. Anyone who is within your vicinity or has intimate access to you, particularly your family, becomes crucial to you for drawing closer to Allah ﷻ. Therefore, the first recipients of your mercy ought to be your family.

The Prophet ﷺ expressed this beautifully in a ḥadīth reported by Abū Hurayrah ؓ. He said, "There are four dinars: a dinar which you give to a poor person, a dinar you give to free a slave, a dinar you spend in the path of Allah ﷻ, and a dinar which you spend on your family. The best of them is the dinar which you spend on your family" (al-Adab al-Mufrad 751).

There are times when these realms intersect. Thus, spending on your family may represent both a charity and the maintenance of ties of kinship. Two aims can be achieved simultaneously through this. We must remember, however, that this is not an excuse to indulge in harmful spending habits within the family; rather, it is encouragement towards generosity and kindness with family members, a practice we should all embrace and view as rewarding.

Indeed, the gratification one experiences when providing for a family member differs significantly from that of charity. Whilst charitable giving occupies a clear place within the realms of reward and benevolence, we need to maintain good intentions when supporting our family members. This, of course, extends to gift-giving during Eid as well.

Generosity towards family, guided by custom and a careful assessment of personal means, is typically the norm. Whilst some may exploit this, the principle of generosity towards our family members is of immense importance and contributes to seeking the pleasure of Allah ﷻ.

For the servants of the Most Merciful, their family members are the first to be entitled to their mercy. Let us consider the example of Saʿd ibn Abī Waqqāṣ رضي الله عنه, who fell gravely ill during the conquest of Makkah, to the extent that death seemed imminent. Subḥān Allāh! It is quite remarkable that Saʿd رضي الله عنه not only survived but lived for several decades after the Prophet ﷺ, ultimately spreading Islam to China. However, at that moment, Saʿd رضي الله عنه was sure that he was at death's door. The Messenger of Allah ﷺ visited him and thought similarly.

Believing his end was near, Saʿd رضي الله عنه asked the Prophet ﷺ about the disposing of his considerable wealth, noting that his only heir was his daughter. Saʿd رضي الله عنه narrates, "The Prophet ﷺ came to visit me whilst I was [sick] in Makkah. He said, 'May Allah bestow His mercy on Ibn ʿAfrāʾ (i.e., Saʿd رضي الله عنه).' I asked, 'O Messenger of Allah, may I bequeath all of my wealth (in charity)?' He said, 'No.' I asked, 'Then may I bequeath half of it?' He said, 'No.' I asked, 'One third?' He said, 'Yes, one third, even one third is too much. It is better for you to leave your inheritors wealthy than to leave them poor, begging others, and whatever you spend for the sake of Allah will be considered as a charitable deed, even the handful of food you put in your wife's mouth. Allah may lengthen your age so that some people may benefit through you, and some others be harmed by you'" (Ṣaḥīḥ al-Bukhārī 2742).

This response surprised Saʿd, as the Prophet had consistently encouraged *ṣadaqah* (charity). Being a Prophet of Allah, he followed the tradition of other Prophets by not leaving behind any inheritance. Everything the Prophets left was charity, as no one can inherit wealth from them. Saʿd was not expecting the Prophet to advise him to retain such a significant portion of his wealth despite only having one heir, but the Prophet explained that leaving your inheritors self-sufficient surpasses leaving them impoverished and dependent on others' charity.

The Prophet also suggested that Saʿd might outlive many, with some benefiting from his existence and others suffering. Following this, the Prophet prayed for Saʿd to have a long life. Indeed, Saʿd outlived the Prophet by several decades, bringing immense benefit to the ummah. Not only did he play a major role in taking Islam to China, but he was also pivotal in the conquest of Persia under the command ʿUmar ibn al-Khaṭṭāb ﷺ.

Can one be extravagant in charitable giving? Although the rights of Allah ﷻ are greater than anyone else's, Allah ﷻ instructs us to prioritise repaying debts before donating to His cause. Hence, even with ḥajj, which is an obligation upon us, if a person has an immediate debt—not a recurring, monthly debt—then this becomes the priority.

One should not incur further debt to perform ḥajj or give *ṣadaqah*. The best expression of devotion to Allah ﷻ in such circumstances is practising other forms of *ṣadaqah* that are non-financial in nature such as acts of service, volunteering, and helping others. With regard to financial contributions, eliminating one's debts takes precedence over this. Living in debt proves detrimental to everyone, affecting both your spirituality and your relationship with Allah ﷻ. Debt clings to you and stalks you, so one should strive to eliminate it.

Consider also the ḥadīth of the Prophet ﷺ asking the Ṣaḥābah to give wealth for the sake of Allah ﷻ. Zayd ibn Aslam ﷺ narrates, "I hear ʿUmar bin al-Khaṭṭāb ﷺ saying, 'We were ordered by the Messenger of Allah ﷺ to give in charity, and that coincided with a time in which I had some wealth, so I said, 'Today I will beat Abū Bakr ﷺ, if I am ever to beat him.' So I came with half of my wealth, and the Messenger of Allah ﷺ asked, "What did you leave for your family?" I said, 'The same amount.' Abū Bakr ؓ came with everything he had, and the Messenger of Allah ﷺ asked, "O Abū Bakr! What did you leave for your family?" He replied, 'I left them Allah and His Messenger.' I said, "By Allah! I will never be able to beat him to something"" (Jāmiʿ al-Tirmidhī 3675).

It is crucial to understand that this represents the exception, not the norm. The Prophet ﷺ usually would not permit the Companions to donate all of their wealth as *ṣadaqah*, risking harm to their families. He recognised that Abū Bakr ؓ held a unique position with Allah ﷻ —a *maqām* (station) of certainty. This meant that Abū Bakr ؓ would not regret his decision or harm his dependents. Instead, he would maintain his composure, return to the marketplace, earn again, and uphold his healthy financial situation.

Moreover, when Abū Bakr ؓ declared, "I am giving you everything, O Messenger of Allah, and I have left Allah and His Messenger for my family", it indicated his complete trust in his capacity to rebuild his wealth and remain financially secure. Abū Bakr ؓ was an exception.

Consider, by contrast, the ḥadīth of Abū Ṭalḥah ؓ, who donated his orchards to the Prophet ﷺ after hearing the *āyah*:

لَنْ تَنَالُوا الْبِرَّ حَتَّىٰ تُنْفِقُوا مِمَّا تُحِبُّونَ ۚ وَمَا تُنْفِقُوا مِنْ شَيْءٍ فَإِنَّ اللَّهَ بِهِ عَلِيمٌ

***You will never attain virtuous conduct until you give from what you love. Whatever you give away, Allah knows about it. [Āl ʿImrān 3:92]***

Or consider, the well-known ḥadīth of Kaʿb ibn Mālik ﵁ who, upon the announcement of his repentence being accepted, wished to give everything for the sake of Allah ﷻ. In both cases, the Prophet ﷺ advised leaving something for their families. He told Abū Ṭalḥah ﵁ to leave some property for his closest relatives, and he suggested that Kaʿb ﵁ hold onto some of his possessions and not become overly excited. Kaʿb ﵁ even gave the shirt off his back in his joy at the acceptance of his *tawbah*!

Therefore, if you choose to donate, it is best to limit your contribution to half of your wealth, rather than emulating Abū Bakr ﵁ and giving it all. This is not an order—there is no obligation to donate half of your wealth for the sake of Allah ﷻ —but rather a general principle one should bear in mind. And if one's financial means to donate are limited, there are plenty of other ways to help—be that through volunteering or even one's positive character.

# Chapter Five Summary

وَالَّذِينَ إِذَا أَنْفَقُوا لَمْ يُسْرِفُوا وَلَمْ
يَقْتُرُوا وَكَانَ بَيْنَ ذَٰلِكَ قَوَامًا

*"And [they are] those who, when they spend, do so not excessively or sparingly but are ever, between that, [justly] moderate..." (25:67)*

## How is moderate spending defined?

- An overlooked element of *tazkiyah* (spirituality) is an awareness of your own consumption and finances.
- Financial moderation is a balance between the two extremes of extravagance and stinginess.
- The Prophet ﷺ said about moderate spending: "That is *hikmah*."
    - *Hikmah* (wisdom) in this context implies having a good understanding of balance and self-control.

## What is extravagance in Islam?

*"And don't stretch your hand to the full extent (like a spendthrift), so that you then sit back blamed and empty-handed." (17:29)*

Much of the definition of extravagance is left to judgement, as it can vary by culture, time, and circumstance. However, there are clear elements of extravagance:

- To spend on anything through unlawful means or on unlawful things.

- To live beyond your means even with what is *halal.*
- To spend in *ṣadaqah* (charity) to show off, not for the sake of Allah.
- Doing something noble with an evil intention is even worse than spending above your means.

## Generosity over extravagance

*"And give the relative his right, and [also] the poor and the traveler, and do not spend wastefully. Indeed, the wasteful are brothers to the devils, and ever has Satan been to his Lord ungrateful." (17:26–27)*

There are two types of wasteful spending:

***ISRAF***

Extravagance with the permissible

Not haram in and of itself, but stretches the purpose of halal until it becomes questionable

This may include lavish weddings, cars you can't afford, etc.

***TABDHEER***

Spending on the impermissible

This may mean spending on forbidden things or spending money that was not earned in a halal way

Misuse of blessings to disobey Allah, like Shaytan

## Can you spend too much on your family?

*"A dinar which you give to a poor person, a dinar you give to free a slave, a dinar you spend in the way of Allah, and a dinar you spend on your family - the greatest of these is the one you spend on your family." (Al-Adab Al-Mufrad 751)*

- Stinginess is condemned to the same degree as extravagance.
- The first recipients of your financial and material *raḥmāh* must be your family.
- Spending on your family has the greatest reward, but still needs to be done with *hikmah*.

---

## Can you spend too much on charity?

*"By no means shall you attain righteousness unless you spend (in Allah's Cause) of that which you love..." (3:92)*

- Charity should be given with *hikmah* and within your means.
- Ensure your family is provided for as part of your *ṣadaqah*.
- Repaying debts must be prioritized over financial charity.
- Meanwhile, you can give non-financial *ṣadaqah*: donate your time, knowledge, etc.

## How do healthy spending habits relate to *tazkiyah* (spirituality)?

A person's spending habits are usually indicative of their personality and spiritual state.

| Healthy Spending Habits | Healthy Spirituality (*Tazkiyah*) |
|---|---|
| Live on a budget | Restrict extravagance/ desires in this world. |
| Avoid impulsive shopping | Have patience because "haste is from the devil." [Sunan al-Tirmidhi 2012] |
| Research before you buy things | Avoid *shubuhat* (doubtful matters), and *shahawat* (desires), both are things you avoid with caution. |
| Avoid triggers for spending | Avoid environments and triggers that would lead you to sin. |
| Practice gratitude. Don't buy new things just because of the fear of missing out. | Practice gratitude. When you thank Allah for what you have, Allah will increase you. (14:7) |

## How can we be neither extravagant nor stingy?

### *THINK*

Upholding generosity with family is a part of being among the Ibad *al-Raḥmān*.

How can you make your family the first recipients of your raḥmāh?

### *REFLECT*

What would be considered *israf* within your own circumstance? What recent purchases have you made could you have made do without?

### *REMEMBER*

To spend in ways that are unwise or impermissible is to be ungrateful to Allah for His blessings and sustenance.

### *ACT*

Work on developing a budget. Pay off your debts. Spend within your means Spend in charity. Be balanced and moderate for the sake of Allah.

CHAPTER 6

# Piety and Scrupulousness

وَالَّذِينَ لَا يَدْعُونَ مَعَ اللَّهِ إِلَٰهًا آخَرَ وَلَا
يَقْتُلُونَ النَّفْسَ الَّتِي حَرَّمَ اللَّهُ إِلَّا بِالْحَقِّ وَلَا يَزْنُونَ ۚ
وَمَنْ يَفْعَلْ ذَٰلِكَ يَلْقَ أَثَامًا

***And those who do not implore besides Allah any other deity, and do not kill the soul which Allah has made sacred—except in the pursuit of justice—and do not commit adultery. Whoever does that will face penalties.***
***[al-Furqān 25:68]***

At first glance, this *āyah* may be easily overlooked, with people thinking, "This does not apply to me, for I have never invoked any deity beside Allah ﷻ or committed murder or *zinā* (adultery). Therefore, I am exempt."

However, Allah ﷻ would not include anything in the Qur'ān that does not benefit every reader in some way. If you are guilty of one of the crimes mentioned, it commands your attention. If you are innocent of these crimes, it still requires your focus, as you need to seek the protection of Allah ﷻ from ever being drawn towards them. It compels you to observe the lessons learned from how others fell into those transgressions.

When discussing *ʿibād al-Raḥmān*, we primarily think

of a list of their actions: they walk with humility; they maintain impeccable character even with those who lack good character towards them; they pray well into the night; and they spend modestly and wisely. This list is largely about what they actively do, rather than what they avoid.

It is striking that actions that the *ʿibād al-Raḥmān* avoid are mentioned in the middle of a list of actions that they actively partake in. The scholars suggest that this insertion underscores a crucial point: the *ʿibād al-Raḥmān* do not lead lives of contradiction.

We often encounter seemingly righteous individuals—those who pray and carry themselves with grace and beauty in public spaces. Yet, such appearances can be deceiving. We know the Hypocrites at the time of the Prophet ﷺ would try to appear as if they were doing good. Ḥudhayfah ibn al-Yamān ؓ said, "The Hypocrites of today are worse than those at the time of the Prophet ﷺ, because in those days they used to do evil deeds secretly, but today they do such deeds openly" (Ṣaḥīḥ al-Bukhārī 7113). Both those who hid their evil and those who acted in the open were considered Hypocrites. When away from the eyes of the Muslims, the Hypocrites were shameless. The Prophet ﷺ said, "One of the things people have learned from the words of the earliest prophecy is: if you have no shame, then do what you like" (Sunan Abī Dāwūd 4797).

The consensus amongst scholars is that, through the mention of acts that *ʿibād al-Raḥmān* avoid, we are being informed that they do not lead lives of contradiction. This reminds us of the ḥadīth of Thawbān ﵁, who narrated that the Prophet ﷺ said, "I certainly know people of my nation who will come on the Day of Resurrection with good deeds like the mountains of Tihāmah, but Allah will make them like scattered dust." Thawban ﵁ said, "O Messenger of Allah, describe them to us and tell us more, so that we will not become of them unknowingly." The Prophet ﷺ replied, "They are your brothers and from your ethnicity, worshipping at night as you do, but they will be individuals who, when they are alone, transgress the sacred limits of Allah ﷻ" (Sunan Ibn Mājah 4245).

Regarding *ʿibād al-Raḥmān*, Allah ﷻ says:

وَالَّذِينَ لَا يَدْعُونَ مَعَ اللَّهِ إِلَٰهًا آخَرَ
وَلَا يَقْتُلُونَ النَّفْسَ الَّتِي حَرَّمَ اللَّهُ إِلَّا بِالْحَقِّ وَلَا
يَزْنُونَ ۚ وَمَن يَفْعَلْ ذَٰلِكَ يَلْقَ أَثَامًا

***And those who do not implore besides Allah any other deity, and do not kill the soul which Allah has made sacred—except in the pursuit of justice—and do not commit adultery. Whoever does that will face penalties. [al-Furqān 25:68]***

Allah ﷻ speaks of *tawḥīd*, which is the very antithesis of hypocrisy. This holds particular significance, because the *āyah* was revealed directly to a Makkan society known for associating partners with Allah ﷻ. To invoke Allah ﷻ is to worship Him, as the Prophet ﷺ told us that *du'ā'* (supplication) is a form of *'ibādah*.

In the final *āyah* of Sūrah al-Furqān, Allah ﷻ says:

قُلْ مَا يَعْبَأُ بِكُمْ رَبِّي لَوْلَا دُعَاؤُكُمْ ۖ
فَقَدْ كَذَّبْتُمْ فَسَوْفَ يَكُونُ لِزَامًا

***Say, "What weight would my Lord give you, were it not for your prayer? But you have denied, and it will be inevitable." [al-Furqān 25:77]***

According to Ibn 'Abbās k, the term *du'ā'*—translated here as "prayer"—in this context signifies *'ibādah* in its entirety. Hence, not "imploring" any other deities besides Allah ﷻ may be more comprehensively interpreted as not worshipping anything except for Him.

Allah ﷻ, by specifically identifying these sins, implies that the followers of *al-Raḥmān* are not characterised by these transgressions. It is inevitable that all people will commit sins and mistakes. However, the most virtuous amongst us sinners are those who repent.

In Sūrah al-Najm, Allah ﷻ says:

وَلِلَّهِ مَا فِي السَّمَاوَاتِ وَمَا فِي الْأَرْضِ لِيَجْزِيَ الَّذِينَ أَسَاءُوا بِمَا عَمِلُوا وَيَجْزِيَ الَّذِينَ أَحْسَنُوا بِالْحُسْنَى ۞ الَّذِينَ يَجْتَنِبُونَ كَبَائِرَ الْإِثْمِ وَالْفَوَاحِشَ إِلَّا اللَّمَمَ ۚ إِنَّ رَبَّكَ وَاسِعُ الْمَغْفِرَةِ ۚ هُوَ أَعْلَمُ بِكُمْ إِذْ أَنْشَأَكُمْ مِنَ الْأَرْضِ وَإِذْ أَنْتُمْ أَجِنَّةٌ فِي بُطُونِ أُمَّهَاتِكُمْ ۖ فَلَا تُزَكُّوا أَنْفُسَكُمْ ۖ هُوَ أَعْلَمُ بِمَنِ اتَّقَىٰ

***To Allah belongs whatever is in Heaven and whatever is on earth. He will penalise those who commit evil according to their deeds. And He will reward those who do good with the best. Those who avoid major sins and indecencies—except what is slight—your Lord is of vast forgiveness. He knew you well, ever since He produced you from the earth, and ever since you were embryos in your mothers' wombs. So do not acclaim your own virtue; He is fully aware of the righteous.***

***[al-Najm 53:31-32]***

Thus, whilst *ʿibād al-Raḥmān* may commit minor sins, they refrain from persisting in these sins. They are incapable of living a life of contradiction, and they do not publicise their transgressions.

Publicising sins is considered to be one of the greatest affronts to Allah ﷻ—to disobey Him and be shielded by Him, only to then publicise and take pride in the sin. This is not referring to one who publicises in search of help, but rather one who publicises through pride and arrogance. Allah ﷻ shields such a person, yet they still venture out and expose their transgressions to the world.

In the above *āyah*, Allah ﷻ mentions three distinct sins that the *ʿibād al-Raḥmān* avoid:

وَالَّذِينَ لَا يَدْعُونَ مَعَ اللَّهِ إِلَٰهًا آخَرَ
وَلَا يَقْتُلُونَ النَّفْسَ الَّتِي حَرَّمَ اللَّهُ إِلَّا بِالْحَقِّ وَلَا
يَزْنُونَ ۚ وَمَنْ يَفْعَلْ ذَٰلِكَ يَلْقَ أَثَامًا

***And those who do not implore besides Allah any other deity, and do not kill the soul which Allah has made sacred—except in the pursuit of justice—and do not commit adultery. Whoever does that will face penalties. [al-Furqān 25:68]***

Polytheism, murder, and adultery are specified. But even if you are not personally guilty of these, you need to remain engaged. These are the most heinous sins in the eyes of Allah ﷻ, which we know from the ḥadīth of ʿAbdullāh ibn Masʿūd ؓ, who narrated, "I asked the Messenger of Allah ﷺ, 'Which sin is most grievous?' He said, '*Shirk*—that you set up a rival to Allah ﷻ—committing adultery with your neighbour's wife, and killing your child for fear of poverty and him eating alongside you'" (Sunan al-Nasā'ī 4015).

Polytheism is the worst of sins—to equate another with Allah ﷻ, who created you. Adultery and murder come next. Adultery with the wife of one's neighbour is especially abominable as it breaks so many bonds of trust and disrupts entire communities. Murdering one's own child out of a fear of poverty is the most despicable type of homicide due to its implications—not only is it monstrous and evil, but it also shows a lack of understanding of Allah ﷻ as the ultimate source of *rizq* (provision).

We often use extreme examples to highlight the horrific nature of an act. The scholars suggest that Allah ﷻ is appealing to the consciences of the pagans of Makkah. These were all offences that they acknowledged were reprehensible, even if they were actively committing them themselves. They were fully aware these were not noble actions.

The behaviour of these pagans becomes clear when reading a comprehensive work of history, such as *Tafhīm al-Qur'ān*, which includes the history of Makkah and its people, and explains how they regarded their idols.

They did not consider their idols significant; indeed, they showed little concern for them. To them, idols were mere commodities, or items in their inventory.

When circumstances took a turn for the worse or they found themselves in genuine fear, they invoked Allah ﷻ alone, calling upon Him exclusively. When Abrahah invaded Makkah, the Quraysh did not plead with the idols to save them or the Kaʿbah. Instead, they invoked Allah ﷻ. Allah ﷻ says:

أَلَمْ تَرَ أَنَّ الْفُلْكَ تَجْرِي فِي الْبَحْرِ بِنِعْمَتِ اللَّهِ لِيُرِيَكُمْ مِنْ آيَاتِهِ ۚ إِنَّ فِي ذَٰلِكَ لَآيَاتٍ لِكُلِّ صَبَّارٍ شَكُورٍ ۞ وَإِذَا غَشِيَهُمْ مَوْجٌ كَالظُّلَلِ دَعَوُا اللَّهَ مُخْلِصِينَ لَهُ الدِّينَ فَلَمَّا نَجَّاهُمْ إِلَى الْبَرِّ فَمِنْهُمْ مُقْتَصِدٌ ۚ وَمَا يَجْحَدُ بِآيَاتِنَا إِلَّا كُلُّ خَتَّارٍ كَفُورٍ

***Have you not seen how the ships sail through the sea, by the grace of Allah, to show you of His wonders? In this are signs for every patient, thankful person. And when waves, like canopies, cover them, they call upon Allah, sincere in their devotion to Him. But when He delivers them safely to land, some of them waver. None denies Our revelations except the ungrateful traitor. [Luqmān 31:32]***

These pagans would casually swap their idols as they desired, stating, for instance, “I no longer find this idol appealing; let me introduce a new one.” They would accessorise the idols as they wished, trading and selling their deities. Allah ﷻ draws our attention to the fact that when in distress, people naturally call upon Him. Even the pagan Arabs—who opposed the monotheism of the Prophet ﷺ—called upon Allah ﷻ when in difficulty.

The pagan Arabs also knew that *zinā* (adultery) was far from noble, even though they engaged in it. The story of the idols placed at *al-Ṣafā* and *al-Marwah* epitomises this. These idols were representations of a man and woman who committed *zinā* within the Kaʿbah and were transformed into stone by Allah ﷻ as punishment. Consequently, they were disgraced and mocked.

Nevertheless, various forms of *zinā* were prevalent amongst the Arabs. Exchanging spouses and committing incest were common. Despite their awareness of the reprehensible nature of these actions and the lack of any benefit for individuals or society, they persisted.

These pagans understood that murder was wrong, even as they killed for trivial reasons. Therefore, the direct mention of *shirk*, adultery, and murder was a wake-up call—however much they wished to avoid the reality, they knew that they were committing evil.

Allah ﷻ tells us that *ʿibād al-Raḥmān* are far removed from these evil practices, and society flourishes as a result. There is mercy in such a society. People do not kill in the name of their idols or commit *zinā*, victimising the more vulnerable party in the relationship and any children born as a result.

The three sins mentioned directly oppose the three major *maqāṣid* (objectives) of Islamic law: the preservation of religion, life, and honour. When individuals betray these three principles, the societal repercussion is a lack of mercy, leading to cruelty and disgrace. This disgrace impacts both the transgressor and the transgressed, the murderer and the murdered, the adulterer and those affected by the adultery. Consequently, the society experiences a loss of innocence, honour, lineage, protection, safety, spirituality, and harmony.

We do not aim for a society with only a few shining individuals amongst us, with the rest engaging in evil and disgrace. Rather, we want societies that both function in accordance with these noble ideals and uphold the preservation of religion, life, and honour.

Scholars note that the increasing prevalence of these three types of crime, as well as the mindlessness of their execution, are amongst the most significant minor signs of the Day of Judgement. There are major signs of the Day of Judgement, which will appear when the day is literally imminent, but there are also minor signs indicating its approach.

The Prophet ﷺ spoke of societies descending into normalisation, desensitisation, and mindlessness. He prophesied things that would take place before the Day of Judgement. For example, he predicted that Dawsī women would perform acts of *shirk* around the Kaʿbah through a dance that was promiscuous in nature, stating, "The Hour will not be established until the buttocks of the women of the tribe of Daws move whilst going round Dhī al-Khalaṣah" (Ṣaḥīḥ al-Bukhārī 7116). Dhī al-Khalaṣah was an idol that was worshipped by the Daws tribe.

This act of *shirk* around the Kaʿbah is mindless and hedonistic, transforming *shirk* into a form of celebration. A habitual disregard for all things Divine had become prevalent, leading to the open mockery of Allah ﷻ and anything associated with Him. When nothing is considered sacred, everything becomes part of a materialistic pursuit. Spirituality is consumed by vanity, with people worshipping not from a place of purpose, but as part of a superficial show.

Mindless murder will also become common before the Day of Judgement. The Prophet ﷺ predicted a time when neither killer nor victim would know the reason behind a murder, stating, "By Him in whose hand is my soul, the world will not pass away till a day comes when the killer will not know why he killed, and the one who is killed will not know why he was killed" (Mishkāt al-Maṣābīḥ 5390).

The perpetrators of murder often have no discernible reason for their actions. Mass shootings, a common occurrence in the United States, serve as a poignant example of such mindless violence. At an international level, senseless killing can be seen in unjust governments with oppressive foreign policies—including our own in the United States—which instigate devastating wars. On an individual level, feelings of emptiness can also lead to mindless killing that shatters societies. The Prophet ﷺ referred to this widespread murder as "*al-harj*" (Ṣaḥīḥ al-Bukhārī 7062, 7063).

Mindless *zinā* is also becoming increasingly prevalent. People commit adultery without any regard for the consequences, demonstrating a complete lack of shame. The Prophet ﷺ predicted this too. In such times, the most virtuous individuals can only request that the act be carried out elsewhere, whilst those committing adultery display utter indifference to observers. Meanwhile, those who witness it regularly grow desensitised.

It is important to ponder over this. Some people may be planning to return to their favourite television series on Netflix, Hulu, or other platforms after reading this book. I mention this not to dismiss you, as I understand the reasoning behind it—you might decide to look away during certain scenes or skip them entirely. But consider the potential corruption of the soul and heart that takes place in this process. You may become desensitised to such acts, viewing them as commonplace. And through this, mindless *zinā* becomes a societal norm, as people grow increasingly desensitised to various forms of immorality, including watching such acts. Consuming content can have detrimental effects not only on the heart but also on the soul.

Allah ﷻ mentioned three extreme acts of sin, and many people may feel distanced from these warnings, thinking, "I have never murdered anyone, committed *zinā*, or committed *shirk*, so these warnings do not apply to me." Yet, it is crucial to remember that no one plans to grow up to be a murderer or to harm others. Many who have taken another life unjustly never anticipated being in such a situation. However, when trials intensify, individuals may find themselves in places they never expected.

Many people believe they will never commit *zinā*, thinking such actions are beneath them and only for others. Yet, they may find themselves becoming too close to their colleagues, which can lead to emotional attachments, flirtatious conversations, and the unfolding of an impermissible relationship. They may rationalise their actions, leading to secret meetings on the phone and other violations of trust. Few anticipate making such grave mistakes until they are caught in the midst of them.

The Prophet ﷺ emphasised the importance of maintaining one's faith. Therefore, we ask Allah to keep faith in us and not allow the afflictions of life to affect our faith. We pray that our faith remains unshaken in a world that is increasingly unpredictable and chaotic. The supplication of the Prophet ﷺ—"O Turner of hearts, keep my heart firm upon Your religion" (al-Adab al-Mufrad 683)—is particularly relevant.

The Prophet ﷺ said, "Be prompt in doing good deeds before [you are overtaken by turbulence which would be like] a part of a dark night. [During that period] a man would be Muslim in the morning and a disbeliever in the evening, or he would be a believer in the evening and a disbeliever in the morning, and he would sell his faith for worldly goods" (Ṣaḥīḥ Muslim 118).

This oscillation between faith and disbelief is a dangerous state to be in, yet it happens to people unexpectedly. Therefore, we pray to Allah ﷻ to not let us lose faith, to settle faith in our hearts, to keep our hearts firm, our steps steadfast, and our thoughts pure, and to guide us to the straight path. We beseech Allah ﷻ to hold us to it and to keep us adherent to this faith, Islam, until we meet Him. We pray for the best of our deeds to be our last, asking Allah ﷻ for *ḥusn al-khitām* (a good ending).

People often do not understand how they are lured into evil circumstances, for they can arise insiduously. The scholars of *sulūk* (spiritual wayfaring) state that each of the three sins mentioned above (i.e., polytheism, murder, and adultery) has a unique pathway that leads to it. Though the pathway may vary from person to person, it exists. The pathway to *shirk* is emptiness and a loss of the sweetness of faith. When one loses the sweetness of *īmān*, their souls become weak to the temptations of Shayṭān. The Prophet ﷺ said, "Surely, the faith of one of you will wear out within him, just as a shirt becomes worn out, so ask Allah ﷻ to renew faith in your hearts" (al-Muʿjam al-Kabīr li al-Ṭabarānī 14668).

This worn-out garment metaphor suggests that faith, when not renewed regularly, fades away. Therefore, individuals experience emptiness, which they may seek to fill with things other than Allah ﷻ. These two loves—a love for Allah ﷻ and a love for sin—contradict one another. One of the two must be expelled from a person's heart. Sadly, people often choose to expel love for Allah ﷻ, but it is emptiness that paves the way to such a decision.

For murder, many scholars suggest that anger is the primary trigger. People often commit murder in the heat of the moment, frequently within domestic scenarios. How often does a heated argument or a momentary lapse in control lead to violence against a loved one, unlocking the potential for greater violence? Sometimes, in the midst of these moments, people commit unthinkable acts that then need to be hidden, turning them into murderers. Shayṭān, thus, unlocks the potential for sin.

Without proper control over one's temper, an individual might become abusive. There are many who never imagine they could harm their spouse or children, believing that they are immune to such despicable acts. Yet, in a momentary loss of control, they snap and inflict pain on their loved ones. The practice and behaviour of *ʿibād al-Raḥmān* should guard them against straying down this dark path.

The sin of *zinā* often stems from lust, emptiness, or a quest for validation. Flirtation begins subtly, often unrecognised until it has progressed significantly. Sparks are allowed to fly, eventually igniting a fire. Allah ﷻ advises us:

وَلَا تَقْرَبُوا الزِّنَا ۖ إِنَّهُ كَانَ فَاحِشَةً وَسَاءَ سَبِيلًا

***And do not go near adultery. It is immoral and an evil way. [al-Isrāʾ 17:32]***

Allah ﷻ urges us not to even get close to *zinā*; we need

to place a barrier between ourselves and temptation. When signs of these temptations become apparent, it is wise to retreat, avoiding compromising situations that could lead to a fall.

There are pathways to these major sins which the *ʿibād al-Raḥmān* actively seek protection from, refusing to trivialise these transgressions. As al-Ḥasan al-Baṣrī ﷺ said, "No one fears hypocrisy but a believer, and no one feels safe from hypocrisy but a hypocrite" (al-Jawāb al-Kāfī 1/42). To think that you are incapable of any sin risks complacency. One must establish protective barriers against these sins, cultivating contemplation, reflection, and systems of external accountability to intervene when one approaches a dangerous path.

If one begins to tread a path leading to evil, there are many safety nets that can pull them back, whether they be internal or external. Over time, external safety nets may fail, and the internal ones must exert their influence, asserting, "I do not like the person I am becoming. I am dissatisfied with the quality of my *duʿāʾ*. I am disturbed by the weakening of my faith. I am uncomfortable with the disconnect I feel from Allah ﷻ, the emptiness I experience, the anger issues I struggle with, and the abrupt manner in which I interact with others." Or, "I find myself disliking the inclination to engage flirtatiously with everyone I encounter, be it a grocery store clerk, a co-worker, or a random individual online. The person I am becoming—one who constantly seeks validation from external sources—does not sit well with me."

One must be willing to reshape oneself into a person worthy of being counted amongst the *ʿibād al-Raḥmān*. This transformation requires deep, honest self-reflection. One must acknowledge when one's actions are veering onto the wrong path. After all, it was the *salaf*, the pious predecessors, who feared committing major sins the most, even though they were those least likely to succumb to such transgressions.

Consider the story of Abū Hurayrah رضي الله عنه, the person who relayed the most narrations from the Prophet ﷺ. He sought the protection of Allah ﷻ from thievery and adultery. One may ask why Abū Hurayrah رضي الله عنه of all people, would need to pray for such refuge? Was he not an incredibly pious and noble man? Of course he was. However, Abū Hurayrah رضي الله عنه reminded his students of Iblīs' downfall, and how he fell from grace despite his seemingly unshakeable faith and prior status. The *salaf* did not ridicule those who fell from grace. Instead, they prayed for the protection of Allah ﷻ against a similar downfall, acknowledging their potential to falter as others had. They took these instances as lessons, reinforcing the need to safeguard themselves against similar pitfalls.

The *salaf* had a distinct understanding of what constituted a major sin. As Anas ibn Mālik was passing away, he engaged in a discussion with one of the *tābiʿīn* (the generation of Muslims that immediately followed the Companions). The *tābiʿīn* were known for their noble deeds and exemplary behaviour.

Anas ibn Mālik, a major Companion of the Prophet, addressed this elite group, saying, "You indulge in such actions that are less significant in your eyes than a hair, whilst we used to consider them destructive sins during the lifetime of the Prophet." Whilst a number of the *tābiʿīn* may have surpassed a number of the Ṣaḥābah (Companions) in the amount of good deeds they performed—reading more Qur'ān, praying more, or giving more in charity—the Companions of the Prophet were more vigilant in protecting themselves against sin. What the *tābiʿīn* saw as small sins, the Ṣaḥābah saw as enormities. They had a higher level of *taqwā* (God-consciousness), and their understanding of what constituted a major sin was, thus, very different to the understanding of subsequent generations.

As we reflect on *zinā* in the modern context, we must include not only major *zinā*, but also the minor *zinā* that our eyes and hearts have become accustomed to. We have become desensitised to content that should shake our very cores. May Allah protect us from this subtle degradation of our spiritual sensitivity.

What crucial lessons can we derive from this observation? The more one climbs to the level of the *ʿIbād al-Raḥmān*, the more they fit the description:

وَالَّذِينَ يَبِيتُونَ لِرَبِّهِمْ سُجَّدًا وَقِيَامًا

***And those who pass the night before their Lord, prostrating and standing.* [al-Furqān 25:64]**

They develop stronger personal connections with Allah ﷻ. Consequently, their obsession with gaining the pleasure of Allah ﷻ intensifies. During this process of spiritual elevation, they naturally begin to hold themselves to higher standards than those to which others adhere. Furthermore, they refrain from trivialising sins, recognising the spiritual poison in what others might dismiss as minor misdemeanours.

The Prophet ﷺ specifically cautioned against a dismissive attitude towards sins, saying, "Beware of minor sins. Indeed, they pile upon a man until he is ruined" (Musnad Aḥmad 3808). He also said, "Beware of minor offenses; like people who descend into the bottom of a valley, one comes after another with a log until they [eventually] bake their bread. Truly, when the one who persistently committed minor sins is taken to account for them, they will ruin him" (Musnad Aḥmad 22808).

Imam al-Ghazālī ﵀, delving deeper into this concept, discussed the impact upon the heart of trivialising sins through another metaphor. He likened this phenomenon to the effect of repetitively dropping water on the same spot on a stone until it is eventually shattered. Even though each individual drop seems harmless, the cumulative effect proves devastating. Similarly, minor sins gradually erode our spiritual foundations.

The most common way we trivialise sins in the modern context is by accepting them as regular, unremarkable aspects of our lives. These might be sins of the tongue—backbiting that we dismiss as mere conversation, actions we justify as cultural norms, visual consumption we excuse as entertainment, or even deficiencies in our *ʿibādah* that we rationalise away. We often accept certain actions as being benign aspects of our lives without giving them proper consideration or understanding their spiritual impact.

One may personally commit a sin and perceive it as insignificant, but that is a dangerous mindset to adopt. Saʿīd ibn al-Jubayr ﵀ reported, "A man said to Ibn ʿAbbās ﵄, 'How many major sins are there? Are they seven?' Ibn ʿAbbās ﵄ replied, 'They are closer to seven hundred than only seven, yet there is no major sin if forgiveness if sought, and there is no minor sin if it is committed persistently'" (Tafsīr al-Ṭabarī 9207). This goes to show how important it is to contemplate our actions—even those we consider mundane.

It is crucial to be cautious with minor sins, for they have the potential to severely damage the heart. They can progressively grow and transform into major sins, especially when committed frequently and without a second thought. Remember how these minor sins can be a gateway to graver offences.

However, despite all of this, Allah ﷻ offers us hope. He says:

قُلْ يَا عِبَادِيَ الَّذِينَ أَسْرَفُوا عَلَىٰ أَنفُسِهِمْ
لَا تَقْنَطُوا مِن رَّحْمَةِ اللَّهِ ۚ إِنَّ اللَّهَ يَغْفِرُ الذُّنُوبَ
جَمِيعًا ۚ إِنَّهُ هُوَ الْغَفُورُ الرَّحِيمُ

***Say, "O My servants who have transgressed against their souls: do not despair of the mercy of Allah. Truly, Allah forgives all sins. He is the Forgiving, the Merciful."***
***[al-Zumar 39:53]***

Here, "*asrafū*" signifies exceeding limits, implying that no matter the magnitude of one's transgressions, the door to mercy remains open. Whether the act was as shocking as taking a hundred lives or as seemingly minor as backbiting a single person, the mercy of Allah ﷻ encompasses all. The phrase "*lā taqnaṭū min raḥmat Allāh*" serves as a powerful reminder to never despair of the mercy of Allah ﷻ, for:

إِنَّ اللَّهَ يَغْفِرُ الذُّنُوبَ جَمِيعًا

***Truly, Allah forgives all sins.***
***[al-Zumar 39:53]***

Allah ﷻ assures us that He forgives all sins. This assurance offers hope to those who feel unworthy of the mercy of Allah ﷻ, believing that they have committed too many sins. You have not gone too far, for the mercy of Allah ﷻ surpasses any transgressions you may have carried out.

The following ḥadīth brings forth a new revelation with every reading, so, I urge you to pay close attention. Abū Hurayrah ﵁ reports that the Prophet Muḥammad ﷺ said, "Allah ﷻ created one hundred units of mercy on the day He created the Heavens and the earth. Each one of them can contain all that is between the Heaven and the earth. Of them, He put one on the earth, through which a mother has compassion for her children and animals and birds have compassion for one another. On the Day of Resurrection, He will perfect and complete His mercy" (Riyāḍ al-Ṣāliḥīn 420).

Before Allah ﷻ created it, *raḥmah* (mercy) did not exist. Allah ﷻ, the Originator of all things, including the qualities we possess, created mercy. And from the mercy He created, He apportioned one part out of one hundred for the earth. Consequently, all instances of mercy, whether conveyed by *ʿibād al-Raḥmān* or manifested between animals, believers, or humans, originate from this single portion of mercy. This includes a mother's affection for her child, a Prophet's compassion for his people, and any other expressions of mercy we witness—they all derive from the single portion of mercy that Allah ﷻ revealed and sent down to us.

The implication of this is immense: Allah ﷻ has reserved the other ninety-nine portions of His mercy for the Hereafter. What does it mean that Allah ﷻ saved these portions of mercy? The Prophet ﷺ clarified the meaning, stating that if a disbeliever was aware of all the mercy that Allah ﷻ holds, he would never lose hope of entering Paradise. Just think about the magnitude of these ninety-nine withheld portions of mercy. Even two or three times the mercy of this world would be huge, so imagine ninety-nine times this mercy.

On the other hand, if a believer was aware of all the punishment that resides with Allah ﷻ, he would never presume himself safe from it. This is the balance of hope and fear. The mercy of Allah ﷻ surpasses His wrath; we have only experienced a fraction of His mercy. Every act of mercy that occurs, whether through *ʿibād al-Raḥmān* or otherwise in this world, originates from one part of the mercy of Allah ﷻ. If we were to truly understand this mercy, we would neither exploit it, nor would we permit ourselves to lose hope in Allah ﷻ. Even the most wicked individual would see a light at the end of the tunnel.

# Chapter Six Summary

وَالَّذِينَ لَا يَدْعُونَ مَعَ اللَّهِ إِلَٰهًا آخَرَ وَلَا
يَقْتُلُونَ النَّفْسَ الَّتِي حَرَّمَ اللَّهُ إِلَّا بِالْحَقِّ وَلَا يَزْنُونَ
وَمَن يَفْعَلْ ذَٰلِكَ يَلْقَ أَثَامًا

*And those who do not implore besides Allah any other deity, and do not kill the soul which Allah has made sacred—except in the pursuit of justice—and do not commit adultery. Whoever does that will face penalties. [al-Furqān 25:68]*

## What does this verse introduce about the *'Ibad al-Raḥmān*?

- Indicates that these are people that don't live a life of hypocrisy.
- Earlier verses described what the *'Ibad al-Raḥmān* do - treat others well, give generously, pray throughout the night, etc.
- This verse describes specifically what they DON'T do - *shirk*, murder, and *zina*.

## Why are these the sins they avoid most?

*"'Abdullah ibn Mas'ud said: 'I asked, "Which sin is worst in the sight of Allah?" He said, "To make any rival to Allah, when He has created you." I asked, "Then what?" He said, "To kill your child for fear that he will eat with you." I asked, "Then what?" He said, "To commit zina with the wife of your neighbour."'" (Bukhari, 8/492)*

- These sins corrupt the soul. They're the worst among all sins.
- Every believer will fall into minor sins, but they do their best to repent and avoid major sins.
- In a society of *'Ibād al-Raḥmān*, there is *raḥmāh* towards people—no dependence on false objects of worship, no victimization of the children of *zina*, no senseless death.

*SHIRK*

(associating partners with Allah)

- Opposite of the Islamic goal of Preservation of Religion.
- "(There will be a period)...a man would be a Muslim in the morning and an unbeliever in the evening, or a believer in the evening and an unbeliever in the morning..." (Sahih Muslim 118)
- The pathway to *shirk* is emptiness—a loss of the sweetness of faith.
- People who are empty seek to fill their emptiness with other than Allah, through dependence on something or someone else, or through outright *shirk*.
- Mindless, widespread *shirk* destroys society and is one of the biggest of the minor signs of the Day of Judgement.

### *MURDER*

- Opposite of the Islamic goal of Preservation of Life.
- "There will come a time when the person who is killing and the person being killed don't know why they are being killed..." (Sahih Muslim 2908)
- The pathway to murder is anger.
- A failure to learn to control your temper can lead to violence.
- Mindless, widespread murder destroys society and is one of the biggest of the minor signs of the Day of Judgement.

### *ZINA*

- Opposite of the Islamic goal of Preservation of Honor
- In Qurayshi society, wife swapping, incest, and similar practices were common, and are becoming common once again.
- The pathway to *zina* is lust, emptiness, and seeking validation.
- It can start off with just flirting, but catches fire at some point. Allah warned us to not even go "near" *zina*
- Mindless, widespread *zina* destroys society and is one of the biggest of the minor signs of the Day of Judgement.

## How did the Pious Predecessors view sins?

*"There is no such thing as a small sin when you insist upon it, and no such thing as a major sin when you seek forgiveness from it." ~ Ibn Abbas*

- Indicates that these are people that don't live a life of hypocrisy.
- Abu Hurairah ﷺ always sought refuge from thievery and adultery. He reminded his students that Iblis thought he was safe from sin too.
- They did not mock those who sinned, but made *du'a* for protection for themselves and others, fearing that they may make the same mistakes.
- Abdullah Ibn Masud ﷺ said, "No one feels safe from hypocrisy except for a hypocrite."
- They didn't belittle sins. They viewed minor sins like the most destructive major sins, since continuous engagement in the same sin may harden your heart.
- They had a healthy balance of hope in Allah's mercy and fear of His punishment.

## How do we become *'Ibād al-Raḥmān* who avoid these transgressions?

> *"Belittling sins is like dripping water on a stone in the same place over and over, until it wears away." - Imam Al-Ghazali*

- If you're experiencing a loss of faith, do whatever you can to maintain it.
- If you feel you're losing control of your anger, take steps to remedy it immediately.
- If you're going on a path of infidelity, completely cut off whatever source is tempting you.
- Develop a connection with Allah that helps you hold yourself to a higher standard.
- Don't accept minor sins as necessary parts of your life or personality.
- Sins between you and Allah: With Allah, only repentance is required for His forgiveness.
- Sins that have caused harm to people: Require a return of rights to the people and your utmost effort to be forgiven by them.

## How do we safeguard ourselves from all types of sins?

*"Oh Turner of Hearts, keep my heart firm on your religion." (Du'ā' of the Prophet ﷺ)*

- Ask Allah to let faith settle in your heart and keep you on the straight path until death.
- Re-forge yourself into an *'Ibād al-Raḥmān* through deep, honest self-reflection.
- Understand that you are capable of sin and put a barrier between you and the sin.
- Avoid the footsteps of Shaytan: don't even approach situations that could lead to sin.

## How do we avoid the actions that are not of the *'Ibād al-Raḥmān*?

*I heard Allah's Messenger ﷺ saying, "Verily Allah created mercy. The day He created it, He made it into one hundred parts. He withheld with Him ninety-nine parts, and sent its one part to all His creatures. Had the non-believer known of all the mercy which is in the Hands of Allah, he would not lose hope of entering Paradise, and had the believer known of all the punishment which is present with Allah, he would not consider himself safe from the Hell-Fire". (Sahih al-Bukhari 6469)*

### *THINK*

What have I normalized in my life without feeling any disturbance in my soul? What sins manifest most often in my life?

### *REMEMBER*

The mercy of a mother to her child, a prophet to his people, a shepherd to his flock, and a kind soul to the entire world is a fraction of Allah's mercy for those who avoid major sins. His mercy overcomes His wrath.

### *REFLECT*

This isn't a *deen* of perfect people. It's a *deen* of imperfect people who will be rewarded so long as they make their best effort. Am I making my best effort to strive for perfection?

### *ACT*

Don't let your tragedy in life be your faith. Develop systems of accountability for yourself. Recognize your triggers. Ask Allah to keep you steadfast in faith.

CHAPTER 7

# Forgiveness and Punishment

يُضَاعَفْ لَهُ الْعَذَابُ يَوْمَ الْقِيَامَةِ وَيَخْلُدْ فِيهِ مُهَانًا ۞
إِلَّا مَنْ تَابَ وَآمَنَ وَعَمِلَ عَمَلًا صَالِحًا فَأُولَٰئِكَ يُبَدِّلُ
اللَّهُ سَيِّئَاتِهِمْ حَسَنَاتٍ ۗ وَكَانَ اللَّهُ غَفُورًا رَحِيمًا ۞
وَمَنْ تَابَ وَعَمِلَ صَالِحًا فَإِنَّهُ يَتُوبُ إِلَى اللَّهِ مَتَابًا

***The punishment will be multiplied for him on the Day of Resurrection, and he will remain in it forever, humiliated. Except for those who repent and believe and perform righteous deeds. These—Allah will replace their bad deeds with good deeds. Allah is ever Forgiving, Most Merciful. Whoever repents and acts righteously has truly returned to Allah in repentance. [al-Furqān 25:69-71]***

Allah ﷻ declares that the punishment for those who commit the major sins of polytheism, murder, and adultery will be multiplied on the Day of Resurrection, and they will endure it in disgrace. Allah ﷻ does not intensify punishment for people beyond what they deserve. When Allah ﷻ discusses punishment on the Day of Judgement, we know that the punishment is exact; one will never be punished for a sin beyond what it warrants. However, when it comes to good deeds,

Allah ﷻ rewards or compensates them in ways we do not deserve.

What does it mean for a punishment to be multiplied on the Day of Judgement? The scholars suggest two distinct implications. It refers to the sins that exist between you and Allah ﷻ, and the sins that occur between you and other individuals. As one of the *salaf* said, "Glad tidings to the one who dies and whose sins perish with them."

It is vital not to leave behind a legacy of harmful actions that continue to afflict others after your death. The above statement encourages people not to carry their sins or harmful deeds into the grave, or inspire harm that persists beyond their demise. Thus, a congratulations is in order to the one who dies and whose sins die with them. Their transgressions are solely between them and Allah ﷻ, for they have not oppressed others.

This is significant because when it comes to being pardoned for a crime committed against Allah ﷻ, there is a single prerequisite, whereas for crimes committed against a person, there are two prerequisites. For crimes against Allah ﷻ, repentance to Him is sufficient. Allah ﷻ says:

إِنَّ اللَّهَ يَغْفِرُ الذُّنُوبَ جَمِيعًا

***Truly, Allah forgives all sins.***
***[al-Zumar 39:53]***

For crimes committed against people, the two prerequisites are: the restoring of the victim's rights to the best of one's ability and forgiveness from whomever was wronged. Sometimes, attempts to rectify wrongdoings may not result in forgiveness from the wronged party, despite one's best efforts. In such cases, the mercy of Allah ﷻ prevails, as He acknowledges the sincerity of the one who committed a crime, even if this sincerity does not yield the desired outcome.

To attain the forgiveness of Allah ﷻ, we must repent. We make *duʿāʾ* to this effect, for example saying; "astaghfiru Allāh wa atūbu ilayh" (I seek the forgiveness of Allah and repent to Him), "Allāhumma innaka ʿafuwwun, tuḥibbu al-ʿafwa faʿfu ʿannī" (O Allah, you are the One who Pardons [and] you love to pardon, so pardon me), and so on. Being forgiven for sins between you and Allah ﷻ is a relatively straightforward process, for Allah ﷻ is al-Ghafūr (the All-Forgiving). We should ask for His forgiveness consistently and sincerely.

In contrast, forgiveness for sins committed against people often proves more challenging, and we frequently neglect such matters. Humans may be vindictive or hold grudges, and we may have violated rights that are difficult to restore.

It is said that the individuals described as having their punishment multiplied on the Day of Judgement due to their major sins are those whose sins fall into both categories: crimes against Allah ﷻ and crimes against people.

Some scholars propose that *"yuḍā'af lahu al-'adhāb"* (the punishment will be multiplied for him) refers to the intensification of punishment, aligning with our previous discussion of the Hellfire as ever-present and all-consuming. It is a terrifying place of severe suffering where one dwells in humiliation. May Allah ﷻ protect us from it. This is the antithesis of an individual honoured in the sight of Allah ﷻ, rather, this is a person who has humiliated themselves.

We must emphasise that in the case of committing a sin against Allah ﷻ, one should not expect forgiveness whilst you persist in that sin. Instead, take steps to establish barriers between yourself and the action. It is inappropriate to implore Allah during the night, saying, "O Allah ﷻ forgive me", without demonstrating a willingness to make changes in your life for His sake. It is improper to invoke His name without showing a desire for forgiveness and mercy, manifested in your striving to do your best in life.

Therefore, if you find yourself on a path leading to faithlessness, sever ties with that course. Terminate any relationship associated with that path before it fully manifests. Establish a complete barrier, erase any related contacts, and turn away from it. Re-evaluate all your relationships. Revisit your marriage. If you are reaching a point where anger and resentment are escalating into violence between you and another, take steps to address this immediately. Do not let the situation escalate to breaking point.

If you are experiencing a loss of faith, invest the necessary time to reaffirm your beliefs. Do not allow your faith to become a mere pastime. Remember the importance of religion in your life. If you feel your faith waning, do everything possible to preserve it.

I pray that Allah ﷾, in His infinite mercy, forgives us and shows us mercy. I pray that Allah ﷾ accepts whatever we offer Him. I implore Allah ﷾ not only to hear our pleas for forgiveness but to enable us to work towards earning His forgiveness. I pray that Allah ﷾, in His boundless Mercy, absolves us of all past sins and grants us the strength and resilience to alter our spiritual trajectory.

I pray that Allah ﷾ replaces our transgressions with good deeds and our bad habits with virtuous ones. I pray for His mercy in this life and the Hereafter. I implore Allah ﷾ to protect us from the punishment of the grave and the Fire, and to grant us all Jannat al-Firdaws. I ask

Allah to help us resolve our grudges and to guide us on the right path in rectifying our misdemeanours, both those against our fellow humans and those against our Creator. Allāhumma āmīn.

After mentioning that the punishment will be multiplied for those who commit *shirk*, murder, and adultery, Allah says:

إِلَّا مَنْ تَابَ وَآمَنَ وَعَمِلَ عَمَلًا صَالِحًا فَأُولَٰئِكَ يُبَدِّلُ
اللَّهُ سَيِّئَاتِهِمْ حَسَنَاتٍ ۗ وَكَانَ اللَّهُ غَفُورًا رَحِيمًا

***Except for those who repent and believe and perform righteous deeds. These—Allah will replace their bad deeds with good deeds. Allah is ever Forgiving, Most Merciful. [al-Furqān 25:70]***

After enumerating the three gravest sins—*shirk*, murder, and adultery—Allah states that for those who repent, believe, and perform righteous deeds; He will transform their evil actions into good ones. Even after one has committed the worst possible sins, Allah continues to extend amnesty, offering the opportunity for repentance and return.

Something striking about this *āyah*, however, is that Allah specifically said:

إِلَّا مَنْ تَابَ وَآمَنَ وَعَمِلَ عَمَلًا صَالِحًا

***Except for those who repent and believe and perform righteous deeds. [al-Furqān 25:70]***

Why does Allah ﷻ mention belief here? Is it not the case that all those who repent to Allah ﷻ necessarily believe in Him? Some scholars aver that *tawbah* (repentance) is mentioned before *īmān* (belief) in this *āyah,* since here, *tawbah* refers to the embracing of Islam, whereas *īmān* refers to the manifestation of Islam. Recall our previous discussion on islām and *īmān*—when they appear together, islām refers to an external reality and *īmān* refers to an internal state.

Other scholars argue that *tawbah* here refers to repentance from major sins that are so severe, their practice is almost like disbelief. The Prophet ﷺ said, "No one who commits *zinā* is a believer at the moment when he is committing *zinā*, no one who drinks wine is a believer at the moment when he is drinking it, no thief is a believer at the moment when he is stealing, and no murderer is a believer at the moment he is murdering" (Sunan al-Nasāʾī 4869). This is not to say the person is legally an unbeliever, but that their action is not that of a believer.

Some scholars propose that *tawbah* precedes *īmān* in this *āyah* because it signifies a turning away from elements that are incompatible with belief. Thus, *tawbah* could be interpreted as either leaving disbelief for Islam or repenting from major sins. These scholars further state that *tawḥīd* is the remedy for *shirk*, establishing the prayer is the remedy for having abandoned the prayer, chastity is the remedy for past *zinā*, and so on. According to their view, for every action that Allah commands one to abstain from, there exists a practical solution.

But the *āyah* tells us something more. It states that Allah will turn the bad deeds of these people into good deeds, which is also something that scholars have debated at length. Does this imply that Allah literally transforms sins into good deeds? Does it mean that Allah allows good deeds to persist whilst eliminating sins when a person enters Islam? Or does it mean that Allah guides one towards beneficial practices in lieu of detrimental ones?

Saʿīd ibn Jubayr said that Allah replaced the idol worship of the pagan Arabs with the worship of Allah, replaced their intimate relationships with disbelievers with lawful marital bonds, and exchanged their acts of aggression against Muslims with acts of solidarity. This is a compelling perspective when contemplating the Makkan context in which the sūrah was revealed. There is a tangible aspect to this as well; whilst infrequent, it is heartening to witness former Islamophobes becoming staunch defenders of Islam, or those who once slandered the Prophet Muḥammad ﷺ becoming his protectors. This is reminiscent of those who battled against the Prophet ﷺ at Badr, only to join forces with him in subsequent conflicts.

Imam al-Ḥasan al-Baṣrī said, "Allah changed their evil deeds to righteous deeds, their *shirk* to sincerity, their wickedness to uprightness, and their disbelief to Islam" (Tafsīr Ibn Kathīr). This gives us hope that we all have the capacity to change for the better.

This interpretation, whilst not the majority opinion, suggests a literal transformation of bad deeds into good deeds, shifting punishment to reward. Even if one does not fully subscribe to this interpretation, it still shows that harmful practices can be replaced with beneficial ones.

Consider, for example, Waḥshī ibn Ḥarb. He was the man responsible for the death of Ḥamzah, the beloved uncle of the Prophet ﷺ. Despite later converting to Islam and seeking forgiveness, he lived with the trauma and guilt of causing such harm to the Prophet ﷺ. The transformation of his actions exemplifies the concept that previous wrongs can be replaced with virtuous deeds.

During the Ḥurūb al-Riddah (Battles of Apostasy), Musaylimah al-Kadhdhāb, a man of vicious disposition who claimed Prophethood, was responsible for the murder of many Companions and *ḥuffāẓ*. Not only did he claim to be a Prophet himself, but he also sought to abolish and abrogate many of the rulings of the Prophet ﷺ. His actions posed a significant threat to the core of Islam, from *rasūl* (Messenger) to *risālah* (Message).

It was Waḥshī رضي الله عنه, as a Muslim, who threw the spear that killed Musaylimah al-Kadhdhāb, who was systematically destroying Islam. Waḥshī acknowledged his actions, stating, "I killed the best of people and the worst of people. This hand took the life of the best of people and the worst of people." This statement is one of redemption, illustrating that Allah ﷻ allows people to recover despite having committed atrocities in the past.

Allah ﷻ says:

إِلَّا مَنْ تَابَ وَآمَنَ وَعَمِلَ عَمَلًا صَالِحًا فَأُولَٰئِكَ يُبَدِّلُ
اللَّهُ سَيِّئَاتِهِمْ حَسَنَاتٍ ۗ وَكَانَ اللَّهُ غَفُورًا رَحِيمًا

***Except for those who repent and believe and perform righteous deeds. These—Allah will replace their bad deeds with good deeds. Allah is ever Forgiving, Most Merciful. [al-Furqān 25:70]***

This *āyah* conveys the unmatched mercy of Allah ﷻ. We mentioned earlier that His mercy is so incomparable to our own that it is forbidden to call anyone else *al-Raḥmān*.

We also mentioned that there are ninety-nine forms of mercy reserved for the Day of Judgement. May Allah ﷻ allow us to experience each of these forms on that day!

Ibn ʿAbbās رضي الله عنهما said, "Their bad deeds are transformed into good deeds. It is not that their previous good deeds remain whilst their bad deeds are simply forgiven. Rather, Allah converts their bad deeds into good deeds." ʿAbdullāh ibn ʿAmr رضي الله عنهما recounts that the Prophet ﷺ said, "A man from my nation will be called before all of creation on the Day of Resurrection, and ninety-nine scrolls will be spread out for him, each one extending as far as the eye can see. Then Allah ﷻ will ask, 'Do you deny any of this?' He will reply, 'No, O Lord.' Allah ﷻ will ask, 'Have My scribes been unfair to you?' Then, He will ask, 'Apart from that, do you have any good deeds?' The man will be terrified and say, 'No.' Allah ﷻ will say, 'Indeed, you do have good deeds with Us, and you will not be treated unjustly this day.' Then, a card will be brought out, upon which is written, 'I bear witness that there is no deity [worthy of worship] but Allah, and that Muhammad is His slave and Messenger.' He will say, 'O Lord, what is this card in comparison to these scrolls?' Allah ﷻ will say, 'You will not be treated unjustly.' Then, the scrolls will be placed on one side of the balance and the card on the other. The scrolls will go up (i.e., weigh less) and the card will go down (i.e., weigh more)" (Sunan Ibn Mājah 4300).

In another ḥadīth, the Prophet ﷺ said, "I know the last of the people of Hell who will be brought forth from it and the last of the people of Paradise to be admitted into it. [It is] a man who will emerge from Hell crawling, and it will be said to him, 'Go and enter Paradise.' He will come to it and it will be made to appear to him as if it is full. Allah ﷻ will say, 'Go and enter Paradise.' He will come to it and it will appear to him as if it is full. So he will say, 'O Lord, I found it full.' Allah ﷻ will say, 'Go and enter Paradise.' He will come to it and it will be made to appear to him as if it is full. So he will say, 'O Lord, I found it full.' Allah ﷻ will say, 'Go and enter Paradise, for you will have the like of the world and ten times more.'" (Sunan Ibn Mājah 4339).

In another narration, Abū Dharr reported, "The Messenger of Allah ﷺ said, 'I surely know the first man who will enter the garden of Paradise and the last man who will emerge from the Fire of Hell. The man will be brought forth on the Day of Resurrection, and the command will be given, "Show him his minor sins, and let his major sins be hidden from him!" He will be told, 'On such-and-such a day, you committed such-and-such and such-and-such sins!' He will acknowledge [these sins] and not disavow them, and he will be fearful of the major sins [that have not been revealed]. Then, the command will be given, "In place of every bad deed he committed, grant him a good deed!" He will say, 'I am guilty of sins that I do not see here!'" Abū Dharr ﷺ also added, "I saw the Messenger of Allah ﷺ smile so broadly that his molar teeth showed!" (al-Shamā'il al-Muḥammadiyyah 228). May Allah ﷻ enable us to witness that smile! Allāhumma āmīn.

The Prophet ﷺ said, "My intercession on the Day of Resurrection will be for those among my nation who committed major sins" (Sunan Ibn Mājah 4310). Subḥān Allāh! What, then, of the person who refrains from major sins? What, then, of the person guilty of only minor sins, the occasional slip-ups, those who always turn back to Allah ﷻ right away?

The magnitude of the mercy of Allah ﷻ is unrivalled and beyond comprehension. Allah ﷻ bestows mercy upon the members of this ummah in abundance. This is the value of the declaration, "*Lā ilāha illā Allāh Muḥammadun Rasūl Allāh*".

Therefore, never let diminished faith devolve into an absence of faith. Regardless of how deeply you sink, do not relinquish the affirmation,"*Lā ilāha illā Allāh Muḥammadun Rasūl Allāh*". This is the foremost declaration, carrying the heaviest weight on the Day of Judgement, surpassing all your deeds, even those performed on Laylat al-Qadr (the Night of Power), your *ṣadaqah* (charity), and your ṣalāh (prayer). Its weight surpasses all—"*Lā ilāha illā Allāh Muḥammadun*

*Rasūl Allāh*". Do not give up this truth, irrespective of how far you fall. May Allah ﷻ protect us all.

As previously mentioned, other scholars argued that the *tawbah* and *īmān* mentioned in the *āyah* are in reference to people leaving disbelief and becoming Muslim. If this is the case, then what does it mean for bad deeds to turn into good ones? What actually happens during this conversion?

Abū Saʿīd al-Khudrī ؓ reported, "The Messenger of Allah ﷺ said, 'If a person accepts Islam, such that his Islam is sound, Allah ﷻ will decree a reward for every good deed that he did before and every bad deed that he did before will be erased. After that will come the reckoning; each good deed will be rewarded [and multiplied] by between ten and seven hundred times. And each bad deed will be recorded as it is, unless Allah, the Mighty and Sublime, forgives it'" (Sunan al-Nasāʾī 4998).

Remarkably, although one of the prerequisites for the acceptance of a good deed is that it be performed for the sake of Allah ﷻ, upon conversion to Islam, Allah ﷻ recognises all the individual's pre-conversion deeds. Allah ensures that these good deeds are not nullified; instead, they are elevated, benefiting the individual in the Hereafter as though they were performed for Him.

Contrastingly, any transgressions the individual may have committed are erased. The Prophet ﷺ then explains that after this process comes al-qiṣāṣ (the reckoning). Each virtuous deed is rewarded tenfold, up to seven-hundredfold, whereas each wrongdoing is recompensed as is, unless Allah ﷻ forgives it entirely. This is yet another display of the boundless mercy of Allah ﷻ.

There are many examples of this phenomenon in action, as many of the Companions of the Prophet ﷺ had committed significant sins before their conversion to Islam. Some of them even struggled with these sins during transition periods, such as when alcohol became prohibited.

Makḥūl narrated, "A very old man with sunken eyes came and said, 'O Messenger of Allah ﷺ, [there is] a man [who] betrayed others and did immoral deeds; there was no evil deed he did not do. If his sins were to be distributed amongst the whole of mankind, they would all be doomed. Is there any repentance for him?' The Messenger of Allah ﷺ asked, "Have you become Muslim?" He said, 'As for me, I bear witness that there is no deity [worthy of worship] but Allah, alone and without partners, and that Muḥammad ﷺ is His servant and Messenger.' The Prophet ﷺ said, "Allah ﷻ will forgive you for whatever you have done and will replace your evil deeds with good deeds." The man said, 'O Messenger of Allah ﷺ, even my betrayals and immoral actions?' The Prophet ﷺ said, "Even your betrayals and immoral actions." The man went away saying, '*Lā ilāha illā Allāh*' and 'Allāhu akbar'" (Tafsīr Ibn Kathīr). The mercy of Allah ﷻ had overwhelmed this man. Several commentators note that he died shortly after this incident.

In Sūrah al-'Ankabūt, Allah ﷻ says:

وَالَّذِينَ آمَنُوا وَعَمِلُوا الصَّالِحَاتِ لَنُكَفِّرَنَّ عَنْهُمْ سَيِّئَاتِهِمْ وَلَنَجْزِيَنَّهُمْ أَحْسَنَ الَّذِي كَانُوا يَعْمَلُونَ

***Those who believe and do good works: We will remit their sins, and We will reward them according to the best of what they used to do. [al-'Ankabūt 29:7]***

Allah ﷻ promises to expiate sins and reward these people according to their best deeds. Allah ﷻ erases all sins, major and minor, through repentance. However, He rewards based on the highest quality of good deeds. Contemplating this, one realises that not only are even the most heinous sins forgiven by Allah ﷻ, but even the smallest positive actions—those that may be noble in intent but fall short in execution—are rewarded in abundance.

In Sūrah al-Aḥqāf, Allah ﷻ says:

أُولَٰئِكَ الَّذِينَ نَتَقَبَّلُ عَنْهُمْ أَحْسَنَ مَا عَمِلُوا وَنَتَجَاوَزُ
عَنْ سَيِّئَاتِهِمْ فِي أَصْحَابِ الْجَنَّةِ ۖ وَعْدَ الصِّدْقِ
الَّذِي كَانُوا يُوعَدُونَ

***Those are they from whom We accept the best of their deeds, and We overlook their misdeeds—among the inhabitants of Paradise—the promise of truth which they are promised. [al-Aḥqāf 46:16]***

Not only does Allah ﷻ forgive, but he replaces our evil with goodness. Allah ﷻ truly is *al-Raḥmān*.

In the passage regarding the servants of the Most Merciful, Allah ﷻ says:

وَمَنْ تَابَ وَعَمِلَ صَالِحًا فَإِنَّهُ يَتُوبُ إِلَى اللَّهِ مَتَابًا

***Whoever repents and acts righteously has truly returned to Allah in repentance. [al-Furqān 25:71]***

Scholars interpret this in several ways. Primarily, when a person sincerely repents to Allah ﷻ, then forgiveness is readily available. Allah ﷻ forgives them entirely from the moment of their sincere repentance. This is an unconditional forgiveness that comes from Allah ﷻ.

However, you should aspire for your repentance to be more than just a moment. You should desire for it to represent a new trajectory, a new page with Allah ﷻ.

This renewed commitment to Allah ﷻ brings about your forgiveness and amnesty. Consider the immense relief experienced by the Companions of the Prophet ﷺ, who had committed numerous transgressions before repenting to Allah ﷻ. However, as the *āyah* above implies, their repentance meant that they substituted bad habits with good ones. Genuine repentance includes replacing the time spent engaging in evil with time dedicated to virtuous pursuits.

ʿUmar ibn al-Khaṭṭāb رضي الله عنه advised, "If you sin against Allah ﷻ in a particular place, do not leave that exact location until you have performed a good deed to replace the sin. This way, that setting will testify for you, not against you, on the Day of Judgement."

During the last ten nights of Ramadan, we often recite the *duʿāʾ*, "O Allah, You are the One who Pardons, Most Generous, and You love to forgive, so forgive me." His forgiveness is connected to His generosity. Not only does He forgive, but He makes attaining rewards easy, exchanging one's evil deeds for good ones.

Allah ﷻ says:

وَهُوَ الَّذِي يَقْبَلُ التَّوْبَةَ عَنْ عِبَادِهِ وَيَعْفُو عَنِ
السَّيِّئَاتِ وَيَعْلَمُ مَا تَفْعَلُونَ

***And it is He who accepts repentance from His worshippers, and remits the sins, and knows what you do. [al-Shūrā 42:25]***

Some may argue that they are undeserving of this mercy. Regardless, Allah ﷻ insists that He accepts the repentance of His servants and overlooks their sins. A person may be overwhelmed by guilt, questioning the extent of their forgiveness. Yet Allah ﷻ reassures them, asserting that He knows their deeds, their true nature, and their efforts to overcome weaknesses.

A mark of sincere repentance lies in whether one has moved beyond the page that Allah ﷻ has erased. If you have sincerely sought His forgiveness, that page of sin has already been erased. However, the true testament to enduring repentance is whether you choose to fill this newly blank page with good deeds.

The Prophet ﷺ said, "Have consciousness of Allah ﷻ wherever you are, follow an evil deed with a good one to wipe it out, and engage people with a wholesome manner" (Jāmiʿ al-Tirmidhī 1987).

If an individual remained cognisant of Allah ﷻ wherever they were, they would avoid sinning completely. It is crucial to distinguish between unintentional errors and deliberate sinning. The Companions of the Prophet ﷺ exemplified *taqwā* (God-consciousness) by navigating through a thicket of thorns. Inevitably, one will get pricked along the way, but the response should be to draw oneself in tighter, heal, and proceed.

*Taqwā* is a holistic concept. It is not tied to a single act, rather, it is an attitude. It should permeate an individual's worship, home life, work life, family relations, and more. *Taqwā* fundamentally involves, to the best of one's ability, avoiding evil in all its forms. The Prophet ﷺ also advised us to counteract a sin with a good deed. After committing a sin, one should follow it up with a virtuous act.

When we falter, it is crucial to ensure that we offset our missteps with virtuous actions. The *ʿibād al-Raḥmān* are not devoid of sin; no person can attain such a state of purity. They are not people who never err. Rather, they are individuals who transform their transgressions into renewed bonds with Allah ﷻ. They take their sins and transmute them into good deeds, using the distance they have felt from Allah ﷻ as a catalyst to strengthen their resolve and draw nearer to Him. The *ʿibād al-Raḥmān* are not individuals incapable of sinning. Rather, they are those who ardently seek the forgiveness of Allah ﷻ when they do.

# Chapter Seven Summary

يُضَاعَفْ لَهُ الْعَذَابُ يَوْمَ الْقِيَامَةِ وَيَخْلُدْ فِيهِ مُهَانًا ۞
إِلَّا مَنْ تَابَ وَآمَنَ وَعَمِلَ عَمَلًا صَالِحًا فَأُولَٰئِكَ يُبَدِّلُ
اللَّهُ سَيِّئَاتِهِمْ حَسَنَاتٍ ۗ وَكَانَ اللَّهُ غَفُورًا رَحِيمًا

*The punishment will be multiplied for him on the Day of Resurrection, and he will remain in it forever, humiliated. Except for those who repent and believe and perform righteous deeds. These—Allah will replace their bad deeds with good deeds. Allah is ever Forgiving, Most Merciful. [25:69-70*

## What does this verse introduce about the *ʿIbād al-Raḥmān*?

- The previous verses mentioned the three worst major sins: *shirk*, murder, and *zina*.
- Allah immediately follows them up with these verses of *raḥmāh*, offering amnesty even after the worst of deeds.
- These verses discuss how the *ʿIbād al-Raḥmān* repent from sins and seek the mercy of Allah.

الرَّحْمَٰن

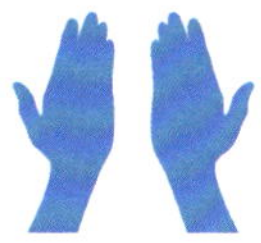

## Why is repentance (*tawba*) mentioned before belief (*amana*)?

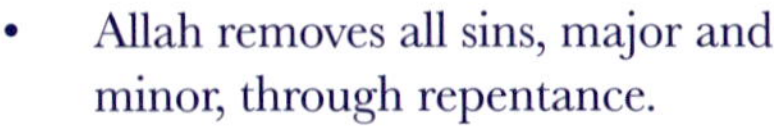

- Allah removes all sins, major and minor, through repentance.
- In order to repent, you must first accept Islam. After repentance, belief in Islam is manifested in the hearts and actions.
    - Islam is an external reality we accept in order to repent.
    - Iman is an internal reality that manifests when belief penetrates the heart.
- Every sin finds a solution in belief:
    - The recourse for *shirk* is *tawheed* (monotheism).
    - The recourse for abandonment of salah is to establish salah.
    - The recourse for *zina* (adultery) is a life of chastity.

---

## What does it mean that Allah exchanges sins for good deeds?

- The *'Ibad al-Raḥmān* are not people who are sinless. They are people who take their slip-ups and turn them into a greater commitment to Allah.
- When a person commits to belief and repents, any good deed from their past will be

preserved, while any sin they committed will be purged.

- After that, each deed will be rewarded 10x up to 700x, and each sin penalized only once, unless Allah forgives those, too.
- The mark of sincere *tawba* is whether you have turned the page that Allah has erased and refilled it with good. Follow up a bad deed with a good deed immediately.
- There is reward in such a change of direction because the same faculties you used to sin are now dedicated to doing good.

## How much *raḥmāh* does Allah have with the believers?

*"A man from my nation will be called before all of creation on the Day of Resurrection, and ninety-nine scrolls [of his sins] will be spread out for him, each one extending as far as the eye can see. Then Allah will say: 'Do you deny anything of this?' He will say: 'No, O Lord.' Then He will say: 'Apart from that, do you have any good deeds?' The terrified man will say, 'No.' (Allah) will say: 'Indeed, you have good deeds with Us, and you will not be treated unjustly this Day.' Then a card will be brought out on which is written [the shahadah]. He will say: 'O Lord, what is this card compared with these scrolls?' He will say: 'You will not be treated unjustly.' Then the scrolls will be placed in one side of the Balance and the card in the other. The scrolls will go up [be light] and the card will [weigh heavily]."– Sunan Ibn Majah 4300*

- This is the value of believing that there is no God but Allah, and that Muhammad ﷺ is His messenger.
- When it comes to Allah's *raḥmāh*, your *shahada* is heavier than all the rest of your five pillars and all your deeds.
- Most of the companions of the Prophet ﷺ had committed major sins before becoming Muslim, yet they had great hope in the *raḥmāh* of Allah.
- Your amnesty is already with Allah; you only need to repent and strive to replace bad habits with good habits.
- Allah is absolutely unmatched in His mercy.
- This and similar hadiths describe mercy for major sins. For those with only minor sins, Allah's mercy will be boundless.

## How do we become *'Ibād al-Raḥmān* who repent and believe?

*"Remember Allah wherever you are, and follow up a bad deed with a good deed, and treat the people with the best of character." [Sunan al-Tirmidhī 1987]*

## *THINK*

No matter how far I'll sink, *la ilaha illa Allah* is the heaviest card on the Day of Judgement. I cannot allow low faith to become no faith. No sin is too large to seek His forgiveness.

## *REFLECT*

Do I recognize Allah as the All-Forgiving, Most Merciful? What do I do after I sin? Do I immediately follow it up with repentance and good deeds in the same area I committed sin? How can I replace my bad habits with good ones?

## *REMEMBER*

Allah is so generous and merciful that in His mercy, He replaces your sins with *hasanat* and wipes them away as if they were never there.

## *ACT*

Be mindful of Allah, wherever you are. Avoid sins, but know that every human sins. Repent to Allah often, and when you slip, follow it up with good.

CHAPTER 8

# Speech and Indecency

وَالَّذِينَ لَا يَشْهَدُونَ الزُّورَ وَإِذَا مَرُّوا بِاللَّغْوِ مَرُّوا كِرَامًا

***And those who do not bear false witness, and when they come across indecencies, they pass by with dignity.***
***[al-Furqān 25:72]***

The *ʿibād al-Raḥmān* maintain their honour, refusing to diminish or degrade themselves by engaging in *shahādat al-zūr* (bearing false witness) or *al-laghw* (futile speech).

If they happen to encounter harmful speech, they pass by with dignity and honour. Allah ﷻ begins with "*al-zūr*", which can have different meanings, one being falsehood. Some scholars interpret this as referring to the most significant falsehood: the rituals of polytheism. These rituals involve honouring and making sacrifices to idols.

Earlier in this passage, Allah ﷻ mentioned that the *ʿibād al-Raḥmān* do not commit *shirk*, murder, or adultery. This sūrah was revealed in Makkah, where polytheism was still rife. Some scholars proposed that this abstention from *al-zūr* refers specifically to refraining from the polytheistic rituals of the time. According to these scholars, the first implication of the phrase "*lā yashhadūna al-zūr*" (they do not witness *al-zūr*) is refraining from these practices. Some scholars extended this to include all major sins, with *shirk* being the pinnacle of *al-zūr*.

Other scholars argued that this phrase refers specifically to *shahādat al-zūr* (false testimony), which the Prophet warned severely against. Another group suggested that it signifies all forms of immorality. The Prophet mentioned those who witness evil, remain silent, and fail to express disapproval. He said, "If people see evil but do not change it, soon Allah will send His punishment upon them all" (Sunan Ibn Mājah 4005).

Tacitly approving evil, or letting it go unchecked, is not a virtue. The Prophet also said, "Whoever believes in Allah and the Last Day should not sit at a table where alcohol is being passed around; whoever believes in Allah and the Last Day should not enter a bathhouse unless he is wearing a waist wrapper; and whoever [amongst the women] believes in Allah and the Last Day should not enter bathhouses [at all]" (Musnad Aḥmad 125).

We do not need to delve deeply into the jurisprudence or potential exceptions to these issues here. The key lesson is that tacit approval signals acceptance to those around you. Even witnessing an act of *ribā* is a crime. Some scholars suggest that "*lā yashhadūna al-zūr*" refers to any witnessing of falsehood, not solely to giving false testimony.

*Shahādat al-zūr* (false testimony) refers to lying in a way that negatively impacts the person against whom the lie is told. This can occur in a court of law, an arbitration situation, or any consequential circumstance, such as alimony negotiations or business contracts. False testimony epitomises *khiyānah* (deception). The Prophet ﷺ said, "There are four (traits)—whoever has them is a hypocrite, and whoever has one of them has one of the traits of hypocrisy, until he gives it up: when he speaks, he lies; when he makes a promise, he breaks it; when he makes a covenant, he betrays it; and when he argues, he resorts to foul language" (Sunan al-Nasāʾī 5020).

False testimony represents a culmination of all that is wrong, for it is not merely a lie. It is a lie with the power to devastate another person's life and results in the violation of their rights. This is the reasoning behind the ḥadīth of Abū Bakrah رضي الله عنه, who recounts that the Prophet ﷺ asked, "Shall I not inform you of the greatest of the major sins?" 'Of course, O Messenger of Allah ﷺ!' the people replied. He said, "Associating partners with Allah, disobeying parents, and false testimony (or false speech)." Abū Bakrah رضي الله عنه added: "The Messenger of Allah ﷺ would not stop repeating it until we said [to ourselves]: 'I wish he would be quiet'" (Jāmiʿ al-Tirmidhī 2301).

This was uncharacteristic of the Prophet ﷺ, indicating the importance he attached to the issue. Imagine if I repeated this phrase for the next thirty minutes: "Beware of false testimony and false speech. Beware of false testimony and false speech. Beware of false testimony and false speech. Beware of false testimony and false speech. Beware of false testimony and false speech." Some of you might wish for me to stop and move on.

*Shirk*, in a way, is a form of false testimony. It is the most extreme form, as one is lying against Allah ﷻ. Bearing false testimony refers to a lie that facilitates oppression or the deprivation of rights. The most egregious form of oppression is when a person fails to acknowledge and fulfil the rights of their Creator. Therefore, the greatest oppression is *shirk*, which negates the right of Allah ﷻ to be worshipped alone.

Ayman ibn Khuraym رضي الله عنه said that the Prophet ﷺ once stood to give a *khuṭbah* and said, "O people, false testimony is tantamount to *shirk* with Allah ﷻ" (Jāmiʿ al-Tirmidhī 2299). Following this, the Messenger of Allah ﷺ recited:

فَاجْتَنِبُوا الرِّجْسَ مِنَ الْأَوْثَانِ وَاجْتَنِبُوا قَوْلَ الزُّورِ

***So shun the abomination of idols, and shun false speech. [al-Ḥajj 22:30]***

Speech and the truth are no trivial matters. In Sūrah al-Mu'minūn, Allāh ﷻ says:

قَدْ أَفْلَحَ الْمُؤْمِنُونَ ۞ الَّذِينَ هُمْ فِي صَلَاتِهِمْ
خَاشِعُونَ ۞ وَالَّذِينَ هُمْ عَنِ اللَّغْوِ مُعْرِضُونَ

***Successful, indeed, are the believers:***
***those who humble themselves in prayer;***
***those who avoid idle talk…***
***[al-Mu'minūn 23:1-3]***

Idle speech can lead to a multitude of unintended consequences. Pressing 'share' on something online means owning it. The act of *naql*, transferring something, equates to the act of *shahādah*, bearing witness to it; and thus, owning it. Subḥān Allāh! The repercussions of sharing information, especially if it is unverified, can be serious.

Such shared information can have major consequences on people's lives. People press share without considering the consequences. The Prophet ﷺ said, "It is enough of a lie for someone to narrate everything they hear" (Ṣaḥīḥ Muslim 5). This refers to mindlessly parroting everything one hears, even if a person does not intend to deceive. This is what *qawl al-zūr* (idle talk) refers to, and it is most evident in a courtroom trial or during a formal procedure where a person is asked to testify.

However, it is crucial to acknowledge that people's lives, honour, and dignity are exposed in the public sphere too. As well as formal courtrooms, we have the court of public opinion. Those who disseminate false information and bear false witness must take responsibility for that. When meeting Allah ﷻ, one cannot simply say, "O Allah, I only pressed share", or "O Allah, I just retweeted it". Be prepared to be asked whether you checked the information and what your intention was in engaging with it.

Whilst a person may not be in a courtroom, the relevance of the information they transmit still matters. The question arises: what value does my opinion bear? Some might argue that a transmission of information is not a matter of responsibility, for they are only presenting it for others to examine, but Allah ﷻ mentions the progression leading to *qawl al-zūr*.

As we previously discussed in the context of major sins, there is a pathway that leads to major sins, such as murder, adultery, and *shirk*. These paths are often paved with minor sins or internal voids that eventually lead one astray.

What, then, is the path leading to something as severe as *qawl al-zūr*? In Sūrah al-Ḥujurāt, Allah ﷻ says:

يَا أَيُّهَا الَّذِينَ آمَنُوا لَا يَسْخَرْ قَوْمٌ مِنْ قَوْمٍ عَسَىٰ أَنْ يَكُونُوا خَيْرًا مِنْهُمْ وَلَا نِسَاءٌ مِنْ نِسَاءٍ عَسَىٰ أَنْ يَكُنَّ خَيْرًا مِنْهُنَّ ۖ وَلَا تَلْمِزُوا أَنْفُسَكُمْ وَلَا تَنَابَزُوا بِالْأَلْقَابِ ۖ بِئْسَ الِاسْمُ الْفُسُوقُ بَعْدَ الْإِيمَانِ ۚ وَمَنْ لَمْ يَتُبْ فَأُولَٰئِكَ هُمُ الظَّالِمُونَ

***O you who believe, no group of men should jeer at another, who may after all be better than them; no group of women should jeer at another, who may after all be better than them; do not speak ill of one another; do not use offensive nicknames for one another. Bad is the name of lewdness after faith. Those who do not repent of this behaviour are evildoers.***
***[al-Ḥujurāt 49:11]***

*Ghībah* (backbiting) is characterised by speaking truthfully about someone in a way that they would find offensive. This form of harmful gossip, whilst true, inflicts pain. A person begins by habitually engaging in *ghībah*, then becomes accustomed to gossiping, before finally starts embellishing the truth to make their stories more sensational or impactful. Lying negatively about someone in their absence is slander. The perpetrator has then fallen into *qawl al-zūr*, which carries significant consequences. But the origin of this path was a lack of respect for personal boundaries and a prideful attitude, where one is too preoccupied with belittling others to focus on self-improvement. May Allah ﷻ protect us from such pitfalls.

Allah ﷻ provides guidance on how to avoid this, saying:

وَالَّذِينَ لَا يَشْهَدُونَ الزُّورَ وَإِذَا مَرُّوا بِاللَّغْوِ مَرُّوا كِرَامًا

***And those who do not bear false witness, and when they come across indecencies, they pass by with dignity.***
***[al-Furqān 25:72]***

A literal translation risks losing much of the meaning of this description. Whenever the *ʿibād al-Raḥmān* find themselves amidst idle chatter, they refuse to engage. If they inadvertently encounter indecency or gossip, whether in a gathering, online, or elsewhere, they continue on their way with dignity. They were not searching for these matters, yet they unexpectedly found them.

Imagine that you are participating in a gathering, and the conversation veers towards discussing someone who is not present. Or, you are in a virtual group chat, as is the norm nowadays, and people start discussing another individual. As you scroll through the conversation, you encounter these discussions. The phrase "*marrū bi al-laghw*" (they come across indecencies) encapsulates this scenario—you were not actively seeking the situation you found yourself in, yet it arrived unbidden.

Allah ﷻ commends those who handle such situations with grace and dignity—*marrū kirāman* tells us that they succeed in doing the right thing in a noble manner.

This connects to the earlier *āyah*, in which Allah ﷻ described people who carry themselves with such dignity and honour that even when they are faced with insults from the foolish, they maintain their graceful demeanour, responding with peace. When they witness inappropriate behaviour, they do not engage, especially when it involves someone else. Remember, the servants of the Most Merciful do not lead lives of contradiction. They do not succumb to the temptation of partaking in gossip simply because they are not the subject of the chatter. They understand that it is not worth their time, regardless of whether the gossip is about them or someone else.

The Prophet ﷺ said, "Whoever amongst you sees an evil, he must change it with his hand; if he is unable to do so, then with his tongue; and if he is unable to do so, then with his heart; and that is the weakest form of faith" (Riyāḍ al-Ṣāliḥīn 184). In other words, if you possess the authority to make a change, you should do so. If the evil can be altered, take action. If it can be stopped, halt it. If this is beyond your means, then you should verbalise your disapproval. In other words, do not hesitate to state, "This is unacceptable". You must intervene, whether verbally or in written form, to express your condemnation.

Compare the following two narrations. The Prophet ﷺ said, "Whoever protects his brother's honour, Allah will protect his face from the Fire on the Day of Resurrection" (Jāmiʿ al-Tirmidhī 1931). The Prophet ﷺ also said, "During the Miʿrāj (Ascension), I saw a group of people who were scratching their chests and faces with copper nails. I asked, 'Who are these people, O Jibrīl?' Jibrīl replied, 'These are the people who ate the flesh of others [by backbiting] and trampled people's honour'" (Sunan Abī Dāwūd 1526).

One's "face" is analogous to their reputation, as defaming someone makes it difficult for them to "show their face" in public. Allah declares that anyone who defends their fellow Muslim will have their face safeguarded from the Fire, symbolising their protection from humiliation.

Imagine a gathering where gossip and backbiting are rampant. Amidst the laughter, individuals reveal their ugliest traits, thereby disgracing themselves. Such behaviour is beneath you, as it not only lowers a person's stature in their own eyes, but it also diminishes their standing in the sight of Allah ﷻ. It makes you wonder why many individuals, despite their good qualities, would choose to discredit themselves in such a manner.

Now picture yourself in this gathering, clearly uncomfortable and repulsed by the conversation. You voice your disapproval, expressing that such discussions are inappropriate, or you make it clear that you disagree with the sentiments being expressed.

The person who declares, "This is not acceptable. I am not comfortable with the conversation or the direction it has taken", may initially face resentment. However, with time, the same people who initially rejected them will come to respect them.

Conversely, the one who gossips and backbites will eventually gain a reputation for being chaotic, leading others to distance themselves from him. As a result, people start to look down upon him because they tire of his abusive language and become suspicious of his intentions. Every time they are around him, he talks about someone else, which leads to paranoia.

As the saying goes, "Whoever quotes other people's words to you, know that they quote your words to other people." Whoever backbites others in your presence, know that they backbite you in the presence of others. It is a habit, a spiritual disease. Initially, people might laugh and indulge in the gossip, but eventually, they will perceive the individual as troublesome and grow to dislike him. However, the person who takes a stand and voices his discomfort will come to be respected.

How do I know this? Through a ḥadīth in which the Prophet ﷺ is reported to have said, "Whoever sought the pleasure of Allah though it was displeasing to the people, Allah becomes pleased with them and will make the people pleased with him, and whoever sought the pleasure of the people though it was displeasing to Allah, Allah becomes displeased with him and will make the people displeased with him" (Jāmiʿ al-Tirmidhī 2414).

You may knock the gossip at such a gathering on the head by declaring, "This is unacceptable; it is not an appropriate manner in which to talk about your brother or sister. I feel highly uncomfortable with this, and we should fear Allah ﷻ". In the immediate aftermath, some people might question your actions, asking, "Why did you have to create an awkward situation?" You might even face social consequences, such as being excluded from future events. However, over time, people will develop respect for you, viewing you as someone who is consistently noble and dignified.

One who does this is not a person who merely intervenes when someone they like is the subject of backbiting. Rather, they never backbite or gossip, and they consistently express their disapproval of such actions. “May Allah reward that brother or sister,” others will say, recognising that they do not ignore inappropriate behaviour but rather hold themselves and others to a higher standard.

Starting with their own selves, they do not accept *al-laghw* and they do not engage in gossip and backbiting. These actions, they realise, inevitably lead to slander. This is a recurring theme for *ʿibād al-Raḥmān*—they stay away from the paths that lead to evil acts. Interestingly, this struggle to remain safe from harmful behaviour can be seen as a form of *raḥmah*. It offers mercy to the one who is being backbitten and, remarkably, also extends mercy to those who are initiating the backbiting. This might seem counterintuitive, but it forces those individuals to reconsider their actions and sins and to think twice about engaging in such harmful behaviour.

Consider the story of Imam Aḥmad ibn Ḥanbal, who was known for his propensity to forgive. He forgave everyone, from those who slandered him to those who physically harmed him in prison—even those who ordered his beatings. However, when a young man once approached him, admitting to having backbitten him and asking for his forgiveness, Imam Aḥmad gave an atypical response. He said he would forgive him on the condition that he did not repeat his actions.

Imam Aḥmad's son was taken aback by this conditional amnesty, as his father's usually forgave without strings attached. When questioned by his son, Imam Aḥmad ﷺ explained that his motive was to prevent the young man from repeating his sin. His act of conditional forgiveness was a manifestation of his love for his students and the ummah, and his desire to help them avoid falling back into sin.

Out of love and care for him, the young man was told not to repeat his sin. It set a high bar and made him think twice before engaging in it again. This is how *ʿibād al-Raḥmān* bring mercy to everyone.

# Chapter Eight Summary

وَالَّذِينَ لَا يَشْهَدُونَ الزُّورَ وَإِذَا مَرُّوا بِاللَّغْوِ مَرُّوا كِرَامًا

*And those who do not bear false witness, and when they come across indecencies, they pass by with dignity. [al-Furqān 25:72]*

## What do these verses introduce about the *ʿIbād al-Raḥmān*?

- They are people who do not give witness to or partake in falsehood (*zūr*).
- If they happen to pass by gossip (*al-laghw*), then they pass with honor and dignity.
- They take reminders, critique, and advice as a means to improve themselves and get closer to Allah.

---

## What does "*zūr*" in this verse imply?

*"Abu Bakrah ﷺ reported: The Prophet ﷺ said, '[The worst of major sins] are to commit shirk and to be disobedient to parents.' The Prophet was reclining and he sat up, saying, 'And surely to speak falsely.' He continued to repeat this until we wished he had stopped." (Sahih al-Bukhari 2511)*

- *Zūr* is not just a simple lie. It's a form of oppression.
    - It can devastate someone's life and lead to the confiscation of their rights.
- *Zūr* can imply witnessing any type of immorality without expressing disapproval in some way.
    - Silence with inaction can mean approval.

## What is "*zūr*"?

It can mean falsehood.
The greatest falsehood is *shirk*.

It can mean false testimony.
The greatest false testimony is slander.

It can take the form of gossip (*al-laghw*). The idlest form of speech is gossip.

## *Shirk*

*"...So avoid the uncleanness of idols and distance yourself from zūr." (22:30)*

The previous verses spoke about *shirk* as one of the major sins *'Ibād al-Raḥmān* avoid.

*Shirk*

is a lie that causes you to negate the greatest right: the right of Allah to be worshipped.

*Zūr*

is a lie that brings about the loss of the rights of one of the creation of Allah.

## Slander

*"O you who have believed, let not a people ridicule [another] people; perhaps they may be better than them; nor let women ridicule [other] women; perhaps they may be better than them. And do not insult one another and do not call each other by [offensive] nicknames. Wretched is the name of disobedience after [one's] faith."* (49:11)

**Slander occurs after a pathway of more minor flaws culminate in *zūr*.**

*Sukhriyya* not minding your own business and having a prideful disposition

*Dhann* having a judgmental heart

*Tajassus* developing a spying eye

*Gheebah* waging a gossiping tongue

*Zūr* embellishing gheebah with falsehood - which becomes slander.

---

## Gossip

*"And when they pass by al-laghw [gossip], they pass by with dignity." (25:72)*

- When the *'Ibād al-Raḥmān* come across *al-laghw*, even accidentally:
  - They excuse themselves and make it clear that the words are not welcome.

    *"Whoever among you sees evil, let him change it with his hand. If he is unable to do so, then with his tongue. If he is unable to do so, then with his heart, and that is the weakest level of faith." (Sahih Muslim 49)*

- "The weakest level of faith" doesn't mean to stay put. It means the least you can do is walk away.
- To take a stand is *raḥmāh* for both the one being victimized and the ones gossiping—who may move on from the sin if they receive a reminder.
    - When people gossip and backbite, they disgrace themselves in the sight of Allah—not the person they discuss.

---

## How do *'Ibād al-Raḥmān* combat these vices?

*"And those who, when reminded of the verses of their Lord, do not fall upon them deaf and blind." (25:72)*

- The *'Ibād al-Raḥmān* have an awareness and focus on pleasing Allah.
    - They don't have space in their eyes or ears for gossip, slander, or falsehood.
- When reminded of the verses and guidelines of Allah, they welcome the advice and strive to enact it.
    - It's essential to the soundness of the heart to be able to receive admonition.
- The opposite of looking for people's faults and listening to gossip is listening to and seeing Allah's words in a way that would cause you to get closer to Him.

## How do we become *ʿIbād al-Raḥmān* who use our faculties for good?

*"Whoever seeks the pleasure of Allah by the displeasure of people, Allah will suffice him against the people. Whoever seeks the pleasure of people by the displeasure of Allah, Allah will leave him to the patronage of people." (Sunan al-Tirmidhī 2414)*

***THINK***

How often do I participate in passing on gossip?

Do I routinely share false information uncritically? Do I ensure that my speech is true and necessary?

***REFLECT***

How can I steer myself off the path of *zūr* and back to Allah?

Am I using the faculties He's given me to get close to Him? Or am I misusing them to harm others?

### *REMEMBER*

The path to *zūr* is long and gradual. Take precautions and guard your heart from the dangers of not minding your own business.

---

### *ACT*

Focus your eyes and ears on Allah alone, not on the idle speech around you. Tune in to sources that remind you to have *taqwa*. When you are confronted by any form of immorality, take a stand or walk away.

CHAPTER 9

# Receptivity and Families

وَالَّذِينَ إِذَا ذُكِّرُوا بِآيَاتِ رَبِّهِمْ لَمْ يَخِرُّوا عَلَيْهَا صُمًّا
وَعُمْيَانًا ۞ وَالَّذِينَ يَقُولُونَ رَبَّنَا هَبْ لَنَا مِنْ أَزْوَاجِنَا
وَذُرِّيَّاتِنَا قُرَّةَ أَعْيُنٍ وَاجْعَلْنَا لِلْمُتَّقِينَ إِمَامًا

***And those who, when reminded of their Lord's āyāt, do not fall against them deaf and blind. And those who say, "Our Lord! Give us comfort in our spouses and offspring. And make us a good example for the righteous." [al-Furqān 25:73-74]***

Now, we are told that the *ʿibād al-Raḥmān* do not ignore the *āyāt* of their Lord ﷻ. How does this relate to the previous *āyah*? Scholars describe two connections here. Firstly, these are people who receive critical advice and admonition well. Everyone loves to give *naṣīḥah* (advice), but few people love to receive it. Allah ﷻ indicates that these people, when reminded of His *āyāt*, do not dismiss them.

When they encounter falsehood and vain speech, they pass by with honour and grace. But when someone reminds them of the *āyāt* of Allah ﷻ, they receive the admonition and critique gladly. This was exemplified by ʿUmar ibn al-Khaṭṭāb رضي الله عنه who, despite his dedication to rectifying everything around him, would humbly accept admonishment from anyone. If any person, whether they were a child or tribal chief, said to 'Umar ﷺ, "Fear Allah ﷻ!" he would suddenly shrink with humility and wonder what he had done wrong. His commitment to justice and virtue was a two-way street—his goal was never to be the one admonishing, but rather to honour Allah ﷻ in all contexts.

The *ʿibād al-Raḥmān* are committed to ensuring that the rights Allah ﷻ has bestowed upon creation are not violated. If they inadvertently violate these rights, they want to be informed. They welcome reminders through the *āyāt* of Allah ﷻ.

Some scholars contend that this *āyah* refers to a group of individuals so engrossed in pleasing Allah ﷻ that they have no room for anything that displeases Him. They are deaf to backbiting, slander, and gossip because they are listening intently to the words of Allah ﷻ, positive teachings, and admonition. They are so absorbed in these pursuits that they tune out to anything else, and their attention is too intensely focused to entertain anything that would lead them away from Allah ﷻ.

My mother ﷺ was a prime example of this. After one of her strokes, she became partially deaf. She would sit in a gathering, offering smiles to everyone, but unable to hear what was being said. In the last decade of her life, one would have to raise their voice and repeat themselves several times in order for her to hear. Yet, she would sit there smiling at everyone and saying, "Al-Ḥamdulillāh! Al-Ḥamdulillāh! I cannot hear the backbiting or gossip anymore!" She expressed a sense of relief, grateful that she could attend events without having to listen to the negative chatter she was once accustomed to. "Al-Ḥamdulillāh," she would say, "Allah ﷻ has shielded me from hearing the usual rubbish." You see, she was tuned in to something else, experiencing something different.

This is a trait of the *ʿibād al-Raḥmān*. Allah ﷻ says:

أُولَٰئِكَ الَّذِينَ أَنْعَمَ اللَّهُ عَلَيْهِمْ مِنَ النَّبِيِّينَ مِنْ ذُرِّيَّةِ آدَمَ وَمِمَّنْ حَمَلْنَا مَعَ نُوحٍ وَمِنْ ذُرِّيَّةِ إِبْرَاهِيمَ وَإِسْرَائِيلَ وَمِمَّنْ هَدَيْنَا وَاجْتَبَيْنَا ۚ إِذَا تُتْلَىٰ عَلَيْهِمْ آيَاتُ الرَّحْمَٰنِ خَرُّوا سُجَّدًا وَبُكِيًّا

***These are some of the Prophets whom Allah has blessed, from the descendants of Ādam, and from those We carried with Nūḥ, and from the descendants of Ibrāhīm and Isrāʾīl, and from those We guided and selected. Whenever the revelations of the Most Gracious were recited to them, they would fall down, prostrating and weeping.***
***[Maryam 19:58]***

When they hear the *āyāt* of *al-Raḥmān*, they are physically humbled and taken to a place of internal connection with Allah ﷻ, causing them to weep. These individuals attentively listen to His words and admonitions, which is the antithesis of seeking out people's faults and indulging in gossip about them. They listen to His words in such a way that it prompts self-improvement—refining oneself for the sake of the Creator—instead of being consumed by irrelevant matters. This is crucial for both the heart and soul. Indeed, a sound heart is key in receiving and internalising the words of Allah ﷻ.

To truly comprehend the words of Allah ﷻ and receive admonition effectively, one must adopt a certain orientation and focus, and avoid anything that corrodes noble values. Allah ﷻ says:

أَفَلَمْ يَسِيرُوا فِي الْأَرْضِ فَتَكُونَ لَهُمْ قُلُوبٌ يَعْقِلُونَ
بِهَا أَوْ آذَانٌ يَسْمَعُونَ بِهَا ۖ فَإِنَّهَا لَا تَعْمَى الْأَبْصَارُ
وَلَٰكِن تَعْمَى الْقُلُوبُ الَّتِي فِي الصُّدُورِ

***Have they not journeyed through the earth and had hearts to reason with or ears to listen with? It is not the eyes that go blind but the hearts, within the chests, that go blind.*** ***[al-Ḥajj 22:46]***

We pray that Allah ﷻ protects us from becoming people whose faculties of hearing, sight, and perception are attuned to that which displeases Him. We pray that Allah ﷻ counts us among those who utilise the faculties for knowing and drawing closer to Him. We seek forgiveness from Allah ﷻ for the times we have misused the blessings of sight, speech, and hearing to disobey Him, rather than the purpose for which He bestowed them upon us, which is to better understand Him.

Allah ﷻ then says:

وَالَّذِينَ يَقُولُونَ رَبَّنَا هَبْ لَنَا مِنْ أَزْوَاجِنَا وَذُرِّيَّاتِنَا قُرَّةَ
أَعْيُنٍ وَاجْعَلْنَا لِلْمُتَّقِينَ إِمَامًا

***And those who say, "Our Lord! Give us comfort in our spouses and offspring. And make us leaders of the righteous." [al-Furqān 25:73-74]***

Indeed, the most distinctive characteristic of the *ʿibād al-Raḥmān* is their profound eagerness for His mercy, most notably manifested in their prayers for salvation.

Earlier, Allah ﷻ acknowledged their pleas for their own safekeeping:

وَالَّذِينَ يَقُولُونَ رَبَّنَا اصْرِفْ عَنَّا عَذَابَ جَهَنَّمَ ۖ إِنَّ عَذَابَهَا كَانَ غَرَامًا

***And those who say, "Our Lord! Avert the suffering of Hell from us! Its suffering is continuous. [al-Furqān 25:65]***

Their sincerity is palpable as they shed tears, earnestly beseeching Allah ﷻ to grant them salvation. They then extend their prayers to their spouses, children, and the righteous in general.

As previously mentioned, those closest to you are most deserving of witnessing the beauty of your character. One way you can exhibit exemplary character to your family is by making *du'ā'* for them. In the depths of the night, the *du'ā'* that you offer for your family is a unique prayer. This is the call for forgiveness for your parents and guidance and blessings for your spouses and children, mirroring the blessings you desire for yourself.

It is critical here to visualise the context in which these *āyāt* were revealed. For most of the Companions in Makkah making this *du'ā'*, their spouses and children had not yet embraced Islam. The noble Ṣaḥābah, a community of converts, implored Allah ﷻ: "O Allah, guide our families. O Allah, guide our spouses. O Allah, guide our children."

These were people who had grown deeply attuned to the reality of the Hereafter and who held immense love and empathy for their families. As they read about the potential torment some will face in the Hereafter, they ardently hoped for their families to avoid such a fate—perhaps even more so than for themselves, for we often love our family, especially our children, more than we love ourselves.

The Ṣaḥābah whose spouses or children had yet to embrace Islam called upon Allah ﷻ, despite their loved ones' continued commitment to idolatry and oppression, pleading, "O Allah, let them be the coolness of our eyes. O Allah, let us witness the moment they embrace Islam."

This is the concept of *daʿwah*, encapsulated by the adage: one cannot give what one does not possess. The servants of the Most Merciful, already steeped in prayer and an understanding of the Hereafter, wish to share this reality with their families. Yet, one of the quickest ways to alienate one's family from Islam is through religious hypocrisy. Hence, these individuals strive to ensure their families witness their exemplary character and how they conduct themselves as *ʿibād al-Raḥmān*, not just in their private prayer practices, but also in their public interactions.

By adhering to a specific regimen and upholding high standards in both worship and work, in private and in public, individuals inspire admiration in the hearts of those who are close to them and observe their sincerity. These inspiring individuals ardently pray, "O Allah, guide our spouses. O Allah, guide our offspring. O Allah, guide our parents." Some of these early Muslims came from a generation whose parents threatened to engage in hunger strikes until they renounced Islam. Imagine a mother declaring, "I will go on a hunger strike until you leave Islam." But these early Muslims were converts who desired not to be the only righteous or safe individuals in their households, but to extend this righteousness and safety to every member of their families.

They pray:

وَاجْعَلْنَا لِلْمُتَّقِينَ إِمَامًا

***"And make us leaders of the righteous."***
***[al-Furqān 25:73-74]***

This plea is not for political leadership or leadership associated with vanity, but for a leadership that embodies piety. They ask to be guides of goodness, to lead the way, and to be amongst the *sābiqūn* (forerunners). This contrasts with the idolaters and the oppressors who competed with each other for worldly reasons, engaging in various pernicious practices to ensure their heirs would be amongst the Makkan elite, holding positions of status and wealth. Whilst these individuals were engrossed in worldly rivalries and focused on securing leadership positions for their children in the secular sense, the *ʿibād al-Raḥmān* sought spiritual leadership.

The *ʿibād al-Raḥmān* are concerned with the leadership of *taqwā* (God-consciousness) and piety. Allah ﷻ told us that these are people whose hearing and sight do not become deaf or blind to admonition when they are reminded of the *āyāt* of their Lord ﷻ. They are not egotistic; they are happy to learn.

The Prophet ﷺ narrates the words of Allah ﷻ in a ḥadīth qudsī, "Whoever harms a *walī* of Mine, I declare war upon him. The most beloved thing My slave draws closer to Me with is that which I have enjoined upon him. My slave continues to draw near to Me with superoragatory acts until I love him. When I love him, I become the ear with which he hears, the eye with which he sees, the hand with which he strikes, and the foot with which he walks. If he asks something of Me, I will give it to him, and if he seeks My protection, I will protect him" (Riyāḍ al-Ṣāliḥīn 386).

The *ʿibād al-Raḥmān* only wish to hear and see things that please Allah ﷻ. They want what Allah ﷻ wants for them, as well as the same for their families and loved ones. In the pursuit of faith and righteousness, individuals often yearn for their loved ones to experience the same spiritual enlightenment and clarity that they have found. We see this in the way new converts speak about their non-Muslim relatives, and these moments are incredibly moving and human.

This theme is prevalent throughout the Qur'ān and resonates with a cross-section of our ummah, from Prophets to the most ordinary of believers. In Sūrah al-Aḥqāf, Allah ﷻ says:

وَوَصَّيْنَا الْإِنسَانَ بِوَالِدَيْهِ إِحْسَانًا ۖ حَمَلَتْهُ أُمُّهُ كُرْهًا وَوَضَعَتْهُ كُرْهًا ۖ وَحَمْلُهُ وَفِصَالُهُ ثَلَاثُونَ شَهْرًا ۚ حَتَّىٰ إِذَا بَلَغَ أَشُدَّهُ وَبَلَغَ أَرْبَعِينَ سَنَةً قَالَ رَبِّ أَوْزِعْنِي أَنْ أَشْكُرَ نِعْمَتَكَ الَّتِي أَنْعَمْتَ عَلَيَّ وَعَلَىٰ وَالِدَيَّ وَأَنْ أَعْمَلَ صَالِحًا تَرْضَاهُ وَأَصْلِحْ لِي فِي ذُرِّيَّتِي ۖ إِنِّي تُبْتُ إِلَيْكَ وَإِنِّي مِنَ الْمُسْلِمِينَ

*We have instructed the human being to kindness to his parents. His mother carried him with difficulty, and she delivered him with difficulty. His bearing and weaning take thirty months. Until, when he has reached his prime at the age of forty, he says, "My Lord, enable*

*me to appreciate the blessings You have bestowed upon me and upon my parents,*

***and to act with righteousness, pleasing You. And improve my children for me. I have sincerely repented to You, and I am of those who submit." [al-Aḥqāf 46:15]***

Then, Allah ﷻ provides a contrasting example—an impious and unbelieving child. Allah ﷻ says:

وَالَّذِي قَالَ لِوَالِدَيْهِ أُفٍّ لَكُمَا أَتَعِدَانِنِي أَنْ أُخْرَجَ وَقَدْ خَلَتِ الْقُرُونُ مِنْ قَبْلِي وَهُمَا يَسْتَغِيثَانِ اللَّهَ وَيْلَكَ آمِنْ إِنَّ وَعْدَ اللَّهِ حَقٌّ فَيَقُولُ مَا هَٰذَا إِلَّا أَسَاطِيرُ الْأَوَّلِينَ

***As for him who says to his parents, "Enough of you! Are you warning me that I will be raised up—when generations before me have passed away?" Whilst they cry to Allah for help, "Woe to you! Believe! The promise of Allah is true!" But he says, "These are nothing but tales of the ancients." [al-Aḥqāf 46:17]***

This individual rejects whatever his parents brought him, and his arrogance means that he does not reason logically. He speaks harshly to them and chastises them, even though all they want is the best for him and they cause him no harm.

Consider the joy of Ibrāhīm ﷺ as he stands with his son Ismāʿīl ﷺ next to the Kaʿbah. Think of his emotions when he made the *du'ā'* that Allah ﷻ has informed us of:

وَإِذْ قَالَ إِبْرَاهِيمُ رَبِّ اجْعَلْ هَٰذَا الْبَلَدَ آمِنًا وَاجْنُبْنِي وَبَنِيَّ أَنْ نَعْبُدَ الْأَصْنَامَ ۝ رَبِّ إِنَّهُنَّ أَضْلَلْنَ كَثِيرًا مِنَ النَّاسِ ۖ فَمَنْ تَبِعَنِي فَإِنَّهُ مِنِّي ۖ وَمَنْ عَصَانِي فَإِنَّكَ غَفُورٌ رَحِيمٌ ۝ رَبَّنَا إِنِّي أَسْكَنْتُ مِنْ ذُرِّيَّتِي بِوَادٍ غَيْرِ ذِي زَرْعٍ عِنْدَ بَيْتِكَ الْمُحَرَّمِ رَبَّنَا لِيُقِيمُوا الصَّلَاةَ فَاجْعَلْ أَفْئِدَةً مِنَ النَّاسِ تَهْوِي إِلَيْهِمْ وَارْزُقْهُمْ مِنَ الثَّمَرَاتِ لَعَلَّهُمْ يَشْكُرُونَ ۝ رَبَّنَا إِنَّكَ تَعْلَمُ مَا نُخْفِي وَمَا نُعْلِنُ ۗ وَمَا يَخْفَىٰ عَلَى اللَّهِ مِنْ شَيْءٍ فِي الْأَرْضِ وَلَا فِي السَّمَاءِ ۝ الْحَمْدُ لِلَّهِ الَّذِي وَهَبَ لِي عَلَى الْكِبَرِ إِسْمَاعِيلَ وَإِسْحَاقَ ۚ إِنَّ رَبِّي لَسَمِيعُ الدُّعَاءِ ۝ رَبِّ اجْعَلْنِي مُقِيمَ الصَّلَاةِ وَمِنْ ذُرِّيَّتِي ۚ رَبَّنَا وَتَقَبَّلْ دُعَاءِ ۝ رَبَّنَا اغْفِرْ لِي وَلِوَالِدَيَّ وَلِلْمُؤْمِنِينَ يَوْمَ يَقُومُ الْحِسَابُ

***And recall that Ibrāhīm said, "O my Lord, make this land secure, and keep me and my children from worshipping idols. My Lord, they have led many people astray. Whoever follows me, he is of me. And whoever disobeys me—You are Forgiving and Merciful. Our Lord, I have settled***

> *some of my descendants in a valley of no vegetation, by Your Sacred House, our Lord, so that they may perform the prayers. So make some people's hearts incline towards them, and provide them with fruits, so that they may give thanks. Our Lord, You know what we hide and what we disclose. And nothing is hidden from Allah, on earth or in the Heaven. Praise be to Allah, Who has given me, in my old age, Ismāʿīl and Isḥāq. My Lord is the Hearer of Prayers. My Lord, make me a performer of prayer, and of my descendants. Our Lord, accept my prayers. Our Lord, forgive me, and my parents, and the believers, on the Day the reckoning takes place." [Ibrāhīm 14:35-41]*

Contrast this with the pain of Nūḥ ﵇ as his son remained behind in the flood. Nūḥ ﵇—who for 950 years spread *daʿwah* and still faced rejection from his wife and son—beseeched Allah ﵁, as we are told in the Qurʾān:

وَقِيلَ يَا أَرْضُ ابْلَعِي مَاءَكِ وَيَا سَمَاءُ أَقْلِعِي وَغِيضَ
الْمَاءُ وَقُضِيَ الْأَمْرُ وَاسْتَوَتْ عَلَى الْجُودِيِّ ۖ وَقِيلَ بُعْدًا
لِّلْقَوْمِ الظَّالِمِينَ ۞ وَنَادَىٰ نُوحٌ رَّبَّهُ فَقَالَ رَبِّ إِنَّ ابْنِي
مِنْ أَهْلِي وَإِنَّ وَعْدَكَ الْحَقُّ وَأَنتَ أَحْكَمُ الْحَاكِمِينَ

***And it was said, "O earth, swallow your waters," and "O sky, clear up." And the waters receded, and the event was concluded, and it settled on [Mount] Jūdī, and it was said, "Away with the wrongdoing people." And Nūḥ called out to his Lord, and said, "O My Lord, my son is of my family, and Your promise is true, and You are the Wisest of Judges."***
***[Hūd 11:44-45]***

He wanted his son to be guided and join him upon the ark, but this was not to be. Imagine the pain he must have felt when his own son had rejected the Message, knowing that he would suffer a terrible fate as a result.

Allah ﷻ also informs us of the advice Yaʿqūb عليه السلام gave his children:

أَمْ كُنْتُمْ شُهَدَاءَ إِذْ حَضَرَ يَعْقُوبَ الْمَوْتُ إِذْ قَالَ لِبَنِيهِ مَا
تَعْبُدُونَ مِنْ بَعْدِي قَالُوا نَعْبُدُ إِلَٰهَكَ وَإِلَٰهَ آبَائِكَ إِبْرَاهِيمَ
وَإِسْمَاعِيلَ وَإِسْحَاقَ إِلَٰهًا وَاحِدًا وَنَحْنُ لَهُ مُسْلِمُونَ

***Or were you witnesses when death approached Yaʿqūb, and he said to his sons, "What will you worship after Me?" They said, "We will worship your God and the God of your fathers Ibrāhīm,***

***Ismāʿīl, and Isḥāq. One God. And to Him, we submit." [al-Baqarah 2:133]***

We all face these challenges. If we have been blessed with Islam, we naturally want to ensure that everyone around us is guided to the truth. This was not unique to the Prophets ﷺ. In fact, it is a form of mercy; we want our families to be safeguarded from harm. Our primary concern is not merely the worldly success of our families, but also their salvation, and this is an expression of our *raḥmah* towards them.

# Chapter Nine Summary

وَالَّذِينَ يَقُولُونَ رَبَّنَا هَبْ لَنَا مِنْ أَزْوَاجِنَا
وَذُرِّيَّاتِنَا قُرَّةَ أَعْيُنٍ وَاجْعَلْنَا لِلْمُتَّقِينَ إِمَامًا

*And those who say, "Our Lord! Give us comfort in our spouses and offspring. And make us a good example for the righteous." [al-Furqān 25:74]*

## What separates the *ʿIbād al-Raḥmān* from the rest of the believers?

- Their most distinctive quality is their eagerness for Allah's *raḥmāh*.
- This eagerness manifests itself in their supplication for salvation.
- But they don't just want *raḥmāh* for themselves—they extend that *raḥmāh* to their families by making *duʿāʾ* for their salvation.

---

## Why is this *duʿāʾ* mentioned in the Qur'an?

- The Sahabah were a generation of converts. In the early Makkan period, they asked for guidance for their families and to best exemplify the faith they'd adopted.

- The best form of *da'wah* is to live your faith and avoid hypocrisy.
- Your character, principles, and your public and private selves are witnesses for or against you.
- Making this *du'ā'* for your family continues to be one of the ways of exemplifying the beautiful character of the *'Ibād al-Raḥmān*. It's a prayer for salvation for those you love most.

## What are the details of this *du'ā'*?

*"Grant us from among our spouses and offspring coolness to our eyes…" (25:74)*

- *Qurrata 'ayyun* – coolness of the eyes
- The previous verses referenced those who do not become deaf or blind to the call of their Lord. Here, believers request that the joy of their eyes be synchronous:
- In the sight of Allah, those with *taqwa* are most deserving of His pleasure.
- In the sight of believers, their joy is to see their families embrace Islam and have *taqwa*.

*"My servant continues to draw near to Me… so that I shall love him. When I love him I am his hearing with which he hears, his seeing with which he sees, his hand with which he strikes and his foot with which he walks." (An-Nawawi 38)*

- Making sincere *duʿāʾ* for families to be guided has been a tradition of all the prophets.
- Ibrahim ﷺ prayed for his sons to believe and establish prayer.
- Yaʿqub ﷺ never stopped praying for Yusuf ﷺ and his other sons.

*"…and make us an example for the righteous."*

- The difference between those who reject faith and the *ʿIbād al-Raḥmān* is this:
- Those who reject faith strive for superiority in worldly pursuits.
- *ʿIbād al-Raḥmān* strive to become the leaders of propagating virtue and piety in the world.

## What is the ultimate reward for embodying all the qualities of *ʿIbād al-Raḥmān*?

*"Those will be awarded the ghurfah (lofty palaces) for what they patiently endured..."*

- *Ghurfah* – literally, the highest room in a multi-story home.
- Similarly, the *ghurfah* is a grand, multi-story palace in the highest level of Heaven.
- It's reserved for the *ʿIbād al-Raḥmān* who struggled the most but embodied excellent character through *sabr* (patience) in all their efforts; with family and those with bad character, with the public, with prayer, and trials, and all other aspects of their lives.

*"I guarantee a house on the outskirts of Paradise for one who leaves arguments even if he is right, and a house in the middle of Paradise for one who abandons lies even when joking, and a house in the highest part of Paradise for one who makes his character excellent." (Sunan Abī Dāwūd 4800)*

*"...and they will be received therein with greetings and [words of] peace." (25:75)*

Paradise will be filled with *salām*.

- It's reserved for the *'Ibād al-Raḥmān* who struggled the most but embodied excellent character through *sabr* (patience) in all their efforts:
- And Allah, the Source of Peace, will greet the people of Paradise with *salām*. [36:58]
- The peace of Paradise will be a reward to the *'Ibād al-Raḥmān* who endured trials with patience.

*'Ibād al-Raḥmān* practice *sabr* (patience) in its most comprehensive sense. They:

- courageously endure their persecution by the enemies of the truth.
- remain firm and steadfast in their struggle to establish Allah's way.
- carry out the duties enjoined by Allah sincerely and tirelessly.
- are not concerned for worldly losses and deprivation.
- withstand all temptations held out by Satan and all the lusts of the flesh.
- make each other patient.

***"And keep yourself patient [by being] with those who call upon their Lord in the morning and the evening, seeking His Face." (18:28)***

*"Peace be upon you for what you patiently endured. And excellent is the final home." (13:24)*

*"Abiding eternally therein. What an amazing abode."*

- What Allah has in store for you in Heaven is better than anything you can have in life due to the natural limitations of the world in which we dwell.
- Even if we had all we wanted here, we would still die.
- Instead of giving you a limited reward in a limited realm, Allah gives you what is unlimited in an unlimited realm.

The Promise of Allah to *'Ibād al-Raḥmān*:

*"There will be an announcer (in Paradise) who will make this announcement: 'Indeed you will be healthy and never sick again. You will dwell here forever and you will not die again, and you will enjoy eternal youth and you will never grow old again, and you will be content in comfort and luxury and you will never face misery or hardship again. And this is the Jannah you have inherited by virtue of the good that you used to do." (Sahih Muslim 2837)*

## How do we become *ʿIbād al-Raḥmān*?

### *THINK*

*Duʿāʾ* is an embodiment of *raḥmāh* to our families. Have I created a daily habit to pray for my families and loved ones to be raised in His sight?

### *REFLECT*

When I struggle with being patient, am I taking time to think of the reward that awaits? Do I strive to be *qurrata a'yun* for my own family?

### *REMEMBER*

A lofty reward in Paradise is granted to the Servants of the Most Merciful. Put it within your sights to encourage you to build habits of *ʿIbād al-Raḥmān*.

### *ACT*

Make *duʿāʾ* for your family and loved ones. The *ʿIbād al-Raḥmān* sincerely believe in the message and are concerned about the faith of their loved ones as much as their own. Long for His *raḥmāh* so you can ultimately dwell in His *raḥmāh*.

CHAPTER 10

# Reward and Bliss

أُولَٰئِكَ يُجْزَوْنَ الْغُرْفَةَ بِمَا صَبَرُوا وَيُلَقَّوْنَ فِيهَا تَحِيَّةً وَسَلَامًا ۞ خَالِدِينَ فِيهَا ۚ حَسُنَتْ مُسْتَقَرًّا وَمُقَامًا ۞ قُلْ مَا يَعْبَأُ بِكُمْ رَبِّي لَوْلَا دُعَاؤُكُمْ ۖ فَقَدْ كَذَّبْتُمْ فَسَوْفَ يَكُونُ لِزَامًا

***It is they who will be awarded the Chamber for having persevered—and will be greeted there with salutations and peace. Remaining in there forever—it is an excellent residence and destination. Say, "What weight would my Lord give you, were it not for your prayer? But you have denied, and it will be inevitable."***
***[al-Furqān 25:75-77]***

The *ʿibād al-Raḥmān* are the ones rewarded with lofty palaces in Paradise for their patience, and they are received in Paradise with respect and greetings of peace.

Here, *taḥiyyah* denotes salutation, honour, and dignity. They are welcomed into Paradise, and given *salām*, the verbal greeting of peace, throughout their stay. Paradise is *Dār al-Salām* (the Abode of Peace). Allah ﷻ says:

جَنَّاتِ عَدْنٍ الَّتِي وَعَدَ الرَّحْمَٰنُ عِبَادَهُ بِالْغَيْبِ ۚ إِنَّهُ كَانَ وَعْدُهُ مَأْتِيًّا ۝ لَا يَسْمَعُونَ فِيهَا لَغْوًا إِلَّا سَلَامًا ۖ وَلَهُمْ رِزْقُهُمْ فِيهَا بُكْرَةً وَعَشِيًّا

***The Gardens of Eden—promised by the Most Gracious to His worshippers in the Unseen. His promise will be fulfilled. They will hear in it no idle speech, but only peace. And they will have their provision in it, morning and evening. [Maryam 19:61-62]***

Both Angels and humans will exchange this greeting in Paradise. Even Allah ﷻ will convey "*salām*":

سَلَامٌ قَوْلًا مِّن رَّبٍّ رَّحِيمٍ

***Peace—a saying from a Most Merciful Lord. [Yā Sīn 36:58]***

The faithful *ʿibād al-Raḥmān* endure insult with patience. They are steadfast in their struggle for the cause of Allah ﷻ, demonstrating patience. They engage in lengthy hours of worship, working tirelessly without worldly concerns, all with patience. They resist temptation—both the temptations of this world and the temptations of Shayṭān—with patience. And they are patient in raising their families according to virtuous principles.

So, when Allah ﷻ decrees:

وَأْمُرْ أَهْلَكَ بِالصَّلَاةِ وَاصْطَبِرْ عَلَيْهَا ۖ لَا نَسْأَلُكَ رِزْقًا ۖ نَّحْنُ نَرْزُقُكَ ۗ وَالْعَاقِبَةُ لِلتَّقْوَىٰ

***And exhort your people to pray, and patiently adhere to it. We ask of you no sustenance, but it is We who sustain you. And the end belongs to reverence.* [Ṭā Ḥā 20:132]**

He is instructing His followers to foster prayer within their families and to exhibit great patience whilst doing so. Allah ﷻ speaks of having patience with those righteous individuals who are scorned in society. It is important to remember that Islam first appealed to the downtrodden, the slaves, the oppressed, and those who did not hail from less privileged backgrounds.

Allah ﷻ says:

وَاصْبِرْ نَفْسَكَ مَعَ الَّذِينَ يَدْعُونَ رَبَّهُم بِالْغَدَاةِ وَالْعَشِيِّ يُرِيدُونَ وَجْهَهُ ۖ وَلَا تَعْدُ عَيْنَاكَ عَنْهُمْ تُرِيدُ زِينَةَ الْحَيَاةِ الدُّنْيَا ۖ وَلَا تُطِعْ مَنْ أَغْفَلْنَا قَلْبَهُ عَن ذِكْرِنَا وَاتَّبَعَ هَوَاهُ وَكَانَ أَمْرُهُ فُرُطًا

***And content yourself with those who pray to their Lord morning and evening, desiring His Attention. And do not turn your eyes away from them, desiring the glitter of this world. And do not obey him whose heart We made oblivious to Our remembrance—so he follows his own whims, and his priorities are confused.* [al-Kahf 18:28]**

The servants of the Most Merciful are patient. They encourage patience amongst each other in the face of any difficulties that come with being part of the Islamic community.

Higher levels in Jannah are awarded to those who are most patient. For example, the Prophet ﷺ is reported to have said, "When a man's child dies, Allah ﷻ asks His Angels, 'Have you taken out the life of the child of My slave?' and they reply in the affirmative. He then asks, 'Have you taken the fruit of his heart?' and they reply in the affirmative. He then asks, 'What did my slave say?' They reply, 'He praised You and said, '*Innā li Allāhī wa innā ilayhī rāji'ūn*' (Indeed, to Allah we belong, and to Him we are returning). Allah ﷻ says: 'Build a house for my slave in Paradise and name it *Bayt al-Ḥamd* (the House of Praise)''" (Riyāḍ al-Ṣāliḥīn 922).

All else being equal, the more hardships one endures in this life, whether inflicted by others or by inexplicable disasters, the higher one's rank in Paradise will be, so long as the person endures these trials with patience.

The Angels will say to the inhabitants of Jannah:

سَلَامٌ عَلَيْكُم بِمَا صَبَرْتُمْ ۚ فَنِعْمَ عُقْبَى الدَّارِ

***"Peace be upon you—because you were patient. How excellent is the Final Home." [al-Ra'd 13:24]***

The salutations the servants of the Most Merciful receive in Paradise are a mark of respect, compensating for the honour they were deprived of in this life due to their humility and character. They endured numerous insults and copiuous derision. However, in the Hereafter, they receive *taḥiyyah* from the Angels. This respect is returned to them as a reward for the *salām* they consistently responded with when faced with challenging situations, such as conciling between believers or responding to the ignorant.

In the face of those who were foolish and tried to provoke them, they replied, "*Salām*." It is only fitting that the *salām* they once extended to others is now returned to them, and by no less than the Angels! Allah ﷻ pronounces:

خَالِدِينَ فِيهَا ۚ حَسُنَتْ مُسْتَقَرًّا وَمُقَامًا

***Remaining in there forever—it is an excellent residence and destination. [al-Furqān 25:76]***

What an extraordinary abode! What an incredible place to settle! What a wonderful residence! And what a remarkable home to rest in for the remainder of your existence!

Recall when Allah ﷻ described the fear the *ʿibād al-Raḥmān* had of Hellfire:

إِنَّهَا سَاءَتْ مُسْتَقَرًّا وَمُقَامًا

***It is a miserable residence and destination." [al-Furqān 25:66]***

The *ʿibād al-Raḥmān* knew that it would be a miserable place to dwell in and a sorrowful setting to endure. Allah ﷻ responds by stating, about Paradise:

خَالِدِينَ فِيهَا ۚ حَسُنَتْ مُسْتَقَرًّا وَمُقَامًا

***It is an excellent residence and destination. [al-Furqān 25:76]***

How subtle, calming, and joyful is the response of Allah ﷻ? You feared the residence of Hellfire, but Allah ﷻ is planning and decorating the residence of Paradise for you. You feared spending time in Hellfire, but Allah ﷻ is admitting you into Paradise for eternity.

This is His response to the *duʿāʾ* made earlier. Allah ﷻ tells us:

وَالْآخِرَةُ خَيْرٌ وَأَبْقَىٰ

***And the Hereafter is better and more lasting. [al-Aʿlā 87:17]***

Whatever Allah has in store for you in the Hereafter surpasses anything that could be presented to you in this life due to the natural limitations of the realm in which we currently dwell.

The enduring nature of the blessings of Allah ﷻ is irrefutable, for they are infinite. Even if Allah were to grant you all your desires in this transient world, the inevitability of death would ultimately dispossess you of them. The love Allah ﷻ has for you extends beyond the provision of temporary pleasures in a finite realm. Instead, Allah ﷻ offers you something boundless in an infinite domain; namely, the reward of Paradise.

This is the gracious response that Allah ﷻ extends to those who invoke Him, fearing not merely the loss of earthly abode, but also the prospect of eternal damnation. May Allah ﷻ shield us all.

The Prophet ﷺ foretold of a herald in Paradise. But before we consider this extraordinary ḥadīth, envisage your first step into Paradise, as you suddenly find yourself in your new celestial palace. As you take in your surroundings, you will question the reality of it all. Subḥān Allāh! For Paradise encompasses that which no eye has witnessed, no ear has heard, and no imagination has ever fathomed. As Jannah unfolds before you, you are guided to your new home.

In this eternal dwelling place, one might look around in awe, uttering, "Subḥān Allāh, is this real?" What, one might ask, is the first announcement made to the inhabitants of Paradise? May Allah ﷻ count us among them!

The Prophet ﷺ narrated that upon entering Paradise and settling into your spectacular, everlasting abode, a resounding proclamation will be made. The Prophet ﷺ said, "When the inhabitants of Paradise enter, an announcer will proclaim, 'You will live therein and never die; you will stay healthy therein and never fall ill; you will stay young and never become old; you will be in a constant state of bliss and never feel miserable'" (Riyāḍ al-Ṣāliḥīn 1892).

In this world, it is not only our surroundings that deteriorate, but our health too. In Paradise, however, we will never lose our vitality. Ageing will be totally absent. Both Paradise itself and its inhabitants remain timeless. You will stay young, never fall ill, and never die. Subḥān Allāh!

How jubilant is this proclamation! In another narration, the Prophet ﷺ said, quoting from the Qurʾān:

وَنُودُوا أَنْ تِلْكُمُ الْجَنَّةُ أُورِثْتُمُوهَا بِمَا كُنْتُمْ تَعْمَلُونَ

***And it will be announced to them, "This is the Garden, awarded to you for what you used to do." [al-Aʿrāf 7:43]***

O Allah, make us amongst those who enter their abode in Paradise without any accountability or punishment, untouched by the Fire. O Allah, allow us to hear this announcement from the herald we have been told about. O Allah, allow us to enjoy these blessings!

Paradise awaits the *ʿibād al-Raḥmān*, may Allah count us among them. May Allah ﷻ envelop us in His mercy. May He continually make us people who yearn for His mercy, and may we convey His mercy to all that surrounds us. May Allah ﷻ grant us the grace to dwell in graves filled with His mercy, be resurrected with His mercy, and dwell eternally in His mercy. And may Allah ﷻ deem us worthy of this lofty title, *ʿibād al-Raḥmān*, servants of the Most Merciful.

# Chapter Ten Summary

وَنُودُوا أَنْ تِلْكُمُ الْجَنَّةُ أُورِثْتُمُوهَا بِمَا كُنْتُمْ تَعْمَلُونَ

*And it will be announced to them, "This is the Garden, awarded to you for what you used to do." [al-Aʿrāf 7:43]*

## What are the Key characteristic of *'Ibad al-Rahman*?

- Prayer.
- Patience.
- Perseverance.
- Steadfastness.

---

## What is the reward for the *'Ibad al-Rahman*?

- Lofty Palaces in Paradise for their patience.
- The greeting of *salām* with great honour, salutations and dignity by Angels.
- They will remain in a constant state of Bliss and never feel miserable.
- Insha Allah ﷻ the greatest reward will be, not to be in Jannah, but to see Allah ﷻ, our Master, our *Rabb*.